Ingersoll In Canada

A Reply To Wendling, Archbishop Lynch, Bystander; And Others

By

Allen Pringle

Ingersoll In Canada

A Reply To Wendling, Archbishop Lynch, Bystander; And Others

by Allen Pringle

ISBN: 978-93-59953-94-6

Published by

DOUBLE 9 BOOKS

2/13-B, Ansari Road
Daryaganj, New Delhi – 110002
info@double9books.com
www.double9books.com
Tel. 011-40042856

ABOUT THE AUTHOR

Allen Pringle's "Ingersoll in Canada" stands as one among his literary masterpieces. A gifted writer, Pringle committed himself to the artwork of ancient analysis, skillfully crafting narratives that bridge the past with the prevailing. Through his phrases, he sought to create connections, encouraging readers to understand and empathize with the human beings, places, and occasions which have shaped records. Pringle's writing is marked through a harmonious combination of creativity and passion. In "Ingersoll in Canada," he invitations readers to explore diverse landscapes and feelings, respiration lifestyles into the historical tapestry of this Canadian city. His narratives are greater than mere money owed; they're windows into the human enjoy, every tale a revelation of the beyond's significance in the gift. What distinguishes Allen Pringle is the fashionable simplicity of his prose. He combines eloquence with accessibility, making his high-quality tales approachable for readers of all backgrounds. His writings are an invitation to adventure via time and region, fostering a deeper appreciation for records's enduring effect on our lives. "Ingersoll in Canada" is a testament to Pringle's dedication to each the craft of storytelling and the venture of connecting humans thru the threads of history.

CONTENTS

PREFACE TO SECOND EDITION

TO THE CLERGY AND COLLEGE STUDENTS OF ONTARIO.

Gentlemen,—Through the generous and voluntary liberality of a highly esteemed and estimable Freethought friend, and at his suggestion, I have been enabled to get out this Second Edition of my pamphlet, of upwards of 4,000 copies, chiefly for gratuitous distribution among yourselves. The gentleman referred to conceived the project of supplying every Minister in the Province with a copy, and it was further decided to also supply the College Students.

The compliment to pamphlet and author, which this action on the part of an intelligent and discriminating Liberal implies, I, of course, duly appreciate. When the work was written a few months ago, at the request of fellow-liberals, I had no expectation that it would ultimately go before so critical and learned a body of readers as the Clergy, Graduates, and College Students of Ontario. I supposed one modest edition of 2,000 copies would be all that would ever see the light. But it has been otherwise desired by my readers. I have, therefore, no further apology to make for presenting you with the work (my object being the advancement of truth), and I earnestly submit for your best consideration its subject matter rather than its literary merits or demerits. The time has come when these great questions must be examined, for they *will* come to the front in spite of the most tenacious conservatism. Everywhere, thoughtful men are earnestly looking into them. That the old landmarks in religious belief are being effaced and the Creeds and Confessions rapidly breaking up is becoming every day more and more apparent. Goldwin Smith, a man of great historical acumen, has recently said "A collapse of religious belief, of the most complete and tremendous kind, is, apparently, now at hand."* The Rev. Hugh Pedley, B.A., Cobourg, in a very able paper in the July (1880) number of the *Canadian Monthly*, on "Theological Students and the Times," says: "There can be no doubt that all forms of thought, all systems of belief, however venerable with age, are being: handled with the utmost freedom. Skepticism is becoming more general, and is protean in its adaptibility to circumstances. There is the philosophical skepticism for the cultured, and popular skepticism for the masses: the Reviews for the select, Col. Ingersoll for the people. No *Index Expurgatorius,* whether Catholic or Protestant, whether ecclesiastical or domestic, is barrier strong enough to stem the incoming tide." He also says: "I would advocate a manly, courageous dealing with the doubts of the age in all our theological schools." * * * "Let there be no timid reserve. Let our young ministers face the whole strength of the rationalistic position." * * * "It is not enough that ministers should be well read in church history, not enough that they should be able to expound in logical fashion the church doctrines of the Trinity, the Atonement, &c, not enough that they should understand the architecture of a model sermon. These matters are quite right in their place, but the minister should go further. He must go down to the root question, and enquire whether the history, the systematic theology, and the homilectics are based on a really Divine Revelation, or only on a series of beautiful legends which foolish, but reverent, hands have wreathed about the person of Jesus of Nazareth, a wonderful, religious genius that long ago illumined the land of Palestine." Further, Mr. Pedley says: "We find men talking as if thoroughness of investigation would inevitably lead to a loosened hold on Christianity. So much the worse then for Christianity. If young men of average intellect, and more than average morality, find that the more keenly they study Christianity, the less able they are to accept it, and preach it, then must Christianity be relegated to the dusty lumber-room of worn-out and superseded religious systems."

* *"The Prospect of a Moral Interregnum."*

—Atlantic Monthly, Nov., 1879.

Mr. Pedley then goes on to point out the effects of ignorance, on the part of the minister, of the arguments and writings of Freethinkers. He says: "If he be pastor in a reading community, he will know less than his congregation about matters which it is his special business to understand. He will stand towards the Bible, as an ignorant Priest stands towards the Pope, accepting an infallibility that he has never proved. He will appear before the intelligent world as a spiritual coward, a craven-hearted man, who dare not face the enemy who is slowly mastering his domains. He will become a by-word and a reproach to the generation which he is confessedly unable to lead, and which sweeps by with disdainful tread, leaving him far in the rear."

These are brave words and frank admissions, which should be well pondered by every clergyman, minister and priest, and every theological student, for should they fail to acquaint themselves with the doctrines and arguments of their opponents, they will speedily find themselves, as Mr. Pedley warns them, preaching to people who know more than they about matters which it is their special business to know.

Yours earnestly for Truth,

A. P. Selby, Nov. 22nd, 1880.

INTRODUCTORY

Col. Robt. G. Ingersoll, the American Freethinker and eloquent iconoclast, visited Canada in April last and lectured on theological subjects in various places, including Toronto, Montreal, Ottawa, Belleville and Napanee, thereby agitating the theological caldron as it has never been agitated before in this country.

And "when Mars was gone the dogs of war were let loose!" Since Ingersoll's departure there has been a profuse shower of "Replies" and "Refutations" from the press, and a tempest of denunciation and misrepresentation from the pulpit. Indeed, before the departure of the redoubtable idol-smasher, the vituperation and slander commenced, under the aegis of "A warning against the Fallacies of Ingersoll." The pious Evangelists of the Y. M. C. A., of Toronto, (abetted doubtless by the clergy) issued this propagandist gospel-manifesto containing slanderous statements against Mr. Ingersoll. This, with much more zeal than courtesy, they thrust upon all entering the Royal Opera House on the first evening of the lectures. The lecturer, in opening, branded the base slander of this Christian document that he (Ingersoll) had signed a petition to allow obscene matter to pass through the mails, as a wilful and malicious falsehood. As this calumny is yet reiterated from press and pulpit, implicating all Freethinkers as being in favor of obscenity, the Resolution on this subject which Col. Ingersoll submitted to the Cincinnati Convention of Freethinkers in September, 1879, will not be out of place here. It was as follows, and passed unanimously:—

Resolved,—That we are utterly opposed to the dissemination through the mails, or by any other means, of all obscene literature, whether inspired or uninspired, holding in measureless contempt its authors, publishers, and disseminators; that we call upon the Christian world to expunge from the so-called sacred Bible every passage that cannot be read without covering the cheek of modesty with the blush of shame.

The cowardly conduct of the Toronto press, with one or two exceptions, in reference to Ingersoll's lectures, was as astonishing to liberal-minded men as it was deplorable to all, especially in the "Queen City of the West," which is, or ought to be, the centre of intellectual activity and progress in Canada. This exhibition of narrow-minded bigotry on the part of the

Toronto press excited (rather unexpectedly to them, no doubt) great surprise and severe animadversion from many quarters. The daily *Globe* and *Mail* have, of course, a very wide circulation, and being the leading newspapers in the country, their numerous patrons look to them for *all* the news on *all* public questions and events. Imagine, therefore, their surprise and indignation on opening their papers and looking for reports of Col. Ingersoll's lectures in Toronto, to find not a word there! Not a syllable by these puritanical publishers is vouchsafed to their expectant patrons, who pay their money for—not merely what suits the religious whims and prejudices of publishers and editors—but for *all* the news. But they would scarcely repeat this mistake—or rather imposition on their readers. They have since unmistakably learned that in this act of pusillanimous servility to the priesthood, they took a false measure of their constituencies; and lamentably failed to gauge correctly the intellectual and moral status of a majority of their patrons.

The honorable exceptions to this servility of the Toronto press, were the *Evening Telegram, Weekly Graphic*, and *National*.

In Belleville, also, there was, I believe, one commendable exception to the narrowness of the press in reference to Ingersoll's lectures. This was the *Free Press*, which has on former occasions proved itself broader than most of its contemporaries.

The Montreal *Canadian Spectator* is another notable exception to this vassalage of the Canadian press; for, though edited by a clergyman, it has proved itself in favor of freedom of speech and liberty of conscience, and boldly denounces the narrow prejudice and bigotry which would gag Ingersoll to-day if it could, and would have burned him two or three centuries ago at the stake.

Chief among the "Replies," and "Refutations" which have issued from the press in Canada since Ingersoll's departure, is that by Hon. Geo. R. Wendling. This honorable gentleman has, for some months past, been shadowing Mr. Ingersoll from place to place with his "reply from a secular stand point;" albeit in Toronto he *preceded* his opponent, and replied (?) before the people of that city to a lecture of Ingersoll's which they had never heard. But, as with the Dutch judge, so with our Christian friends, *one side* of the case was enough to hear in order to be able to give a verdict, and Mr. Wendling was duly applauded for his "satisfactory answer" to the absent heretic!

Subsequently, however, Mr. Ingersoll put in an appearance in the Queen City, and gave his lecture on "The Gods," to which his honorable opponent had replied in advance. This eloquent and argumentative lecture was greeted with such obvious favor and vociferous applause that the "Willard Tract Depository and Bible House" of that city deemed it imperative to do something to counteract the "poisonous" influence that had gone forth. They accordingly hastened forthwith to issue Wendling's "Reply to Robert Ingersoll." This Christian politico-religious *brochure* was heralded by some half dozen Toronto Professors and Doctors of Divinity, and one Vice-Chancellor, to wit: Messrs. McLaren, Rainsford, Potts, Castle, Powis, Antliff and Blake. These gentlemen, in a neat little preface, certify their approval of and admiration for Mr. Wendling's "Reply to the infidelity advocated by Col. Ingersoll," and add the hope that "it may be circulated by thousands."

To this no Freethinker has, of course, any objection, so long as he enjoys an equal right to circulate his documents too. Of this right I propose to avail myself, and briefly review the salient points (if there are any) of some of Ingersoll's Canadian critics. Not that I feel called upon to defend Col. Ingersoll. Should defence be necessary, he is amply able to defend himself. But as our Christian friends, like drowning men catching at straws, have, in their alarm for the safety of their creed, desperately clutched a *layman*, and issued with their unqualified endorsation, this "lay" reply of Mr. Wendling, who comes before the public, he tells us, "as a citizen, as a business man, as a lawyer, and as a politician," and withal as a "man of the world," I have thought that for another layman—a materialistic layman—(though no lawyer or politician) to examine some of Mr. Wendling's lay logic and legal sophistry and politico-religious hash would be a move in the right direction in the interests of truth.

Our Christian friends, in issuing their pamphlet, have very judiciously "improved the occasion" by a liberal sprinkling of admonitory Scripture texts, which adorn the insides of the covers, etc. By these texts we are reminded that "all Scripture is given by inspiration of God," and that "if any man shall add unto these things, God shall add unto him the plagues that are written in this book; and if any man shall take away from the words of the book of this prophecy, God shall take away his part out of the Book of Life," etc., etc. But these, our Christian opponents, are not quite consistent. Verily, the Christian Church is not willing to take its own medicine—the medicine it mixes for "infidels." *We* are warned that if we criticise that book, or take away from the words of it, or ridicule its absurdities, we will surely incur the wrath and "plagues" of an angry God; yet these Christians themselves are complacently doing this very thing. They have already eliminated from its sacred pages infant damnation, and eternal torture; while a "Bible Revision Committee," composed of learned and distinguished dignitaries of different branches of the Christian Church, are now actually engaged in "taking away from the words of this book!"* Consistency! thou art a jewel!! Greg, Strauss, Colenso, Renan, Ingersoll, Underwood, and a thousand others, are consigned to Hades for their destructive criticism of the Christians' Bible; while those learned Christian Doctors of Divinity of the "Revision Committee" can tamper with the "Word of God" and alter it to suit the enlightenment of the age with impunity! They can excise whole passages without incurring the "plagues" we are told shall be visited upon any man who adds to or takes from it.

Now, I have thought if I should adopt the advice contained in the Latin proverb, *fas est ab hoste doceri,* and take a lesson from the ingenious propagandic tactics of our Christian friends in placing conspicuously before their readers choice texts from their Evangelists and Apostles, it may not be amiss. Hence, we, too, will do a little skirmishing with some choice sayings of some of the most eminent and learned apostles of our school. And to those trenchant utterances of Huxley, Tyndall, Mill, Carlyle, etc., herein given, I beg to direct the careful attention of the reader.

To disarm possible criticism, I may say that this little pamphlet has been written by request, amidst a pressure of farm work, in snatches of time intervening between other more imperative duties: and to the advanced Materialist who has gone over the same ground on the different subjects as myself, I may say it is not written for him, as he does not require it. But it is for another class of *quasi* liberals, and Christians who have read Wendling and the others replied to, and are in an inquiring mood after truth. And if the arguments are not wholly *new* I would simply urge in extenuation that there is scarcely anything new under the sun, and also my entire agreement with Montaigne, when he declares he "has as clear a right to think Plato's thoughts as Plato had."

ALLEN PRINGLE.

Selby, Ont., June 25, 1880.

* *The following appears in the press:—"The New Testament Revision Committee have struck out as spurious the last seven verses of the last chapter of St. Mark." Now why have they done this thing? To an "outside barbarian" the true reason would appear to be that according to those seven verses there are no Christians on the earth to-day, as not one from the Pope of Rome or the Archbishop of Canterbury down to the humblest follower of Jesus can prove himself a Christian by the plain test therein given.*

REPLY TO WENDLING

On reading Mr. Wendling's "Reply to Robert Ingersoll," it is difficult to determine precisely its theological status, or what are Mr. Wendling's positions, doctrinally, in reference to Christianity. By the flexibility of doctrine, and dubious orthodoxy, displayed therein, it is no easy matter to *place* Mr. Wendling; and his uncertain positions and theological gyrations remind one of the famous mathematical definition of Infinity—"a sphere whose circumference is everywhere and whose centre is anywhere."

Mr. Wendling says he "champions no creed, no sect," and he assures us he "places humanity above all creeds." Now, Christianity is undoubtedly a creed; albeit, some modern theologians, seeing that the dogmas on which it rests are fast crumbling away, have discovered that Christianity is simply a "life." As to "placing humanity above all creeds," this move is decidedly rationalistic and utilitarian. It is clearly a positive doctrine of the Atheistic philosophy; and it looks more than suspicious that this shrewd lawyer has been "stealing our thunder," for he will find no such doctrine in the Bible, and it certainly has no place in Christian ethics or philosophy. The Bible represents man as below everything else rather than above—"a mere worm of the dust" It represents him as utterly depraved, "deceitful above all things and desperately wicked," and without any good in him. Christianity, instead of holding humanity above all creeds, has, without compunction, immolated man by scores of thousands on the bloody altar of creed and dogma. To maintain its creeds intact, Christianity has reddened the surface of the earth with human blood. Therefore, whatever Mr. Wendling may think about the elevation of man above creeds, Christianity does not hold humanity above its creeds.

With respect to the authenticity and inspiration of the Bible, Mr. Wendling's position is extremely dubious. He tells us that "so much of that book" (the Bible) "as properly records His" (Christ's) "works and truthfully reports His sayings, must be true." But who is to decide which the particular portions are which "properly record" and "*truthfully* report" Christ's works, especially as these "records" and "reports" are self-contradictory, and more especially as nothing was recorded in Christ's time of His sayings or doings, nor until half a century or more after His death, as historical criticism and research abundantly prove? If Mr. Wendling believes the Bible to be an inspired book, wholly authentic and true, the foregoing statement about "so much of it" as "*truthfully* reports," &c, is surely a most extraordinary one. Again, Mr. W. says, "I say so much of that book as bears upon the Ideal Man" (Christ) "and so much of that book as the Ideal Man has set the seal of His approval on, we may accept as the long sought for moral teacher," &c. As before, I would ask, who is to decide what particular part or parts of this book "the Ideal Man has set the seal of His approval on?" or whether the "Ideal Man" ever set His seal upon any of it? or, indeed, whether this "Ideal Man" ever had other than a purely *ideal* or subjective existence in the minds of men? Some able scholars—notably Rev. Robt. Taylor—have, after careful historical research, come to the conclusion that the Christ of the Gospels never existed. But, be this as it may, scholars now generally agree that whether such a person as Jesus of Nazareth lived or not, we have no authentic account of Him; and not a syllable of His alleged sayings was recorded during His alleged lifetime, nor for more than half a century after His death. The reader who wishes to pursue this subject of the wholly unauthentic character of the Gospels, &c, &c, is referred to Greg's "Creed of Christendom," Lord Amberley's "Analysis of Religious Belief," and the great work lately published in England, and now reprinted here by the Messrs. Belford of Toronto, viz., "Supernatural Religion."

It will thus be seen that Mr. Wendling's doctrinal attitude towards the Bible and Christianity is extremely problematical, and a Materialist scarcely knows where to place him, or how to deal with his mongrel positions. Being, as he tells us, "a business man," "a lawyer," "a politician," and "a man of the world," this versatile gentleman has evidently imbibed largely of the utilitarian and humanitarian spirit of the age, while at the same time retaining his Christian predilections; and hence the hybrid homily with which we have to deal, and which he calls a "Reply to Robert Ingersoll from a Secular Standpoint." That a layman, however, should give so uncertain a sound as to his orthodox whereabouts, and, in attempting to defend his positions (whatever they are) and answer Freethinkers, should bring forth such a doctrinal nondescript, is not indeed to be much wondered at, seeing that the clergy themselves, being mercilessly driven from pillar to post by modern science and research, occupy the most inconsistent and incongruous, not to say ridiculous, positions, in doctrine and dogma, in ecclesiastical formulary and Biblical exegesis.

However, though of dubious doctrine and doubtful orthodoxy, some of Mr. Wendling's positions, or rather assumptions and assertions, are clear enough, and not to be misunderstood; and in a few of the more important of these I propose to follow him.

At the outset he dogmatically postulates the assumption that "what most we need is the conviction that there *is* a personal God." From social, commercial, and political considerations this belief in a personal God is what we most need—so says Mr. Wendling. He talks as though, were it not for this theistic belief, everything would go to the dogs; and universal, moral, social and political chaos would come. This, however, is simply assumed without a shadow of proof. He then goes on with his demonstration (?) of the existence of a personal God; but it is the old, old story over again. First he assumes, in the face of the highest authorities to the contrary, that "among every people in every quarter of the habitable globe, there exists, and there has existed from the very furthest reach of history, the idea of one eternal and all-powerful God." He then gives us a rehash of Paley's design argument to prove the existence of a God, which he considers conclusive. And, finally, as if conscious of the weakness of the intellectual argument, he takes refuge in the moral argument,—in conscience in man as showing the existence of a personal God with moral attributes. This is the last refuge of the Theist—the *dernier ressort* of the theologian. Driven utterly from the realm of reason they fly to *conscience* and to *consciousness* to establish subjectively what cannot be proved intellectually. Now, this sort of evidence may do for the Theist and theologian who are determined to believe in Theos; but to those who live in the light of reason, and in the realm of intellect not wholly submerged by the emotions, such inner-consciousness evidence will not be satisfactory; for they experience no such subjective proof in their own minds, and do not care to take the mere *feelings* of others as evidence of anything further than the existence of nervous ganglion and brain.

I will now take up Mr. Wendling's arguments to prove the existence of a personal God, *seriatim,* and briefly consider them. As already remarked, before setting out to prove a God, Mr. W. postulates the necessity of one. For the preservation of moral order, social purity, and commercial integrity, what most we need, it is assumed, "is the conviction that there is a personal God." This assertion certainly has a queer look when we reflect that Theism is at present the prevailing belief among the masses, and has been in the past; and that our prisons are full of persons who believe in a personal God; and that believers in God ascend the gallows almost daily, and are swung off to "mansions in the skies!" Here are some half dozen examples of this kind at hand, the whole of which I quote from one newspaper, a late issue of the Kingston *British Whig*:—

Breaux, who was hanged in New Orleans, "ascended the gallows smiling and said he had made his peace with God and all men." Bolen, who was executed at Macon, Mississippi, said on the gallows: "My mouth will soon be closed in this world. I rested in the arms of Jesus last night. I am satisfied. I feel guilty of nothing. God is well pleased with my soul." Macon, who was executed at the same place, said, "I feel ready to die, because God has pardoned my sins. I risked my soul on the murder, but God has forgiven me. There is not a cloud in the way." Brown, who was also executed at Macon, with the other two, the same day, said, "I have made peace with God, and will surely go to heaven, I will cross the river with a rope around my neck that will lead my wicked soul on to glory. Blessed be God! I am going home!" Stone, who was hanged at Washington, and Tatio at Windsor, Vermont, the same day as the four above, both had made their peace with God, and were on their way "to meet the Lord Jesus Christ."

A belief in God did not it seems avail to keep these men, nor thousands of others, from crime; nor does it, in my opinion, to any great extent, operate as a deterrent of crime. People with favorable organizations and good surroundings will not be apt to commit murder whether they believe or disbelieve in a God; while persons born with, bad organizations—bad heads and impure blood—will very likely, under favorable circumstances, continue to follow their predominant impulses, whether they believe in one God or twenty, and, if Christians in belief, they will ultimately rely on that "fountain of blood open for sin and all uncleanness." Unscrupulous men who have strong natural tendencies to crime, and believe in the Christian plan of salvation, will, in bad surroundings, scarcely fail to indulge their propensities and finally avail themselves of the "bankrupt scheme"—take a bath in that impure fountain and be "washed" clean (?) like the gentry instanced above.

In January and February of this year (1880) Rev. E. P. Hammond, the noted Methodist revivalist, made a professional tour through Canada in pursuit of his favorite and profitable calling of "saving souls" (favorite, probably, *because* profitable). Among other places he visited St. Catharines, and before leaving that city, preached a sermon for the especial benefit, it would seem, of the Universalists. Now, Universalism has always been specially odious to the other more evangelical sects, especially the Methodists, who seem positively shocked at the horrid idea that hell may perhaps be ultimately emptied of its human contents and all mankind get into heaven. The Universalists appear to have a good degree of that noble human quality, benevolence, and hence they believe that the God they worship is too good to damn forever any creature he has made. For this good opinion of their Creator they are duly stigmatized, contemned and reprobated by the ultra orthodox party, who can brook no nonsense about the possibility of the fires of hell ever being extinguished. These people are evidently well pleased at the idea that there is a place of torture into which the non-elect of their fellow creatures may be turned for ever and ever. How like the God of the Old Testament, these disciples of His are! Mr. Hammond, it would seem, is of this class; and accordingly, in the sermon alluded to, proceeded to unbudget himself against Universalism and Universalists in vigorous style. The sermon was reported in the St. Catharines *Journal*, and called forth an able and spirited reply through the same-medium from the Rev. J. B. Lavelle of Fulton, Township of Grimsby. I propose to make some extracts, quite relevant to the subject under consideration, from the reply of Rev. Lavelle,—who is a gentleman, I am informed, of exemplary character and broad intelligence, and highly respected. Mr. Lavelle says:

"Permit me to say, Mr. Editor, in justice to Universalists, both on this continent and in Europe, among whom are some of the ablest Biblical scholars, and some of the best men, that there is not a particle of truth in Mr. Hammond's representation. * * * Mr. Hammond, with other ministers of the endless misery school, believes in the doctrine of 'imputation,' 'substitution,' or 'vicarious' suffering of Christ, which they erroneously, as we think, call the Atonement; and that the greatest villain, who has lived a life of crime, rapine, and murder, can take the benefit of this Spiritual Bankrupt Act (for it is nothing else) at any time before he dies, and 'go to heaven'—yea, even while standing on the gallows, swing 'into glory' and thus escape the consequences of his wicked life.

"For instance, A and B are two consummate villains, and have been so for years, but in a quarrel A murders B—of course B goes to an eternal hell—but, through the labors of Mr. Hammond and others of the so-called orthodox churches who visit him in his cell before his execution—he repents. (?) They lay this Spiritual Bankrupt Act before him. He sees it is the only alternative to keep out of hell; so he takes the benefit of it, is hanged, and goes to heaven. Thus, the murderer gets to heaven by the lucky chance of being the murderer instead of the murdered. If his victim had been fortunate enough to-strike the fatal blow, he could have changed places with him; and so the endless destiny of each would have been reversed by the chance blow of a street fight! Is it, I ask, on such grounds God distributes rewards and punishments? What must be the moral influence of such a doctrine?

"Again: A lives a life of crime for sixty years, and on the very next month or day, repents by taking the benefit of this Spiritual Bankrupt Act, dies and goes to heaven. B lives a life of virtue and goodness for sixty years, and the very next day or month makes a false step, or commits a crime, and is consigned to an endless hell to suffer intense misery without relief and without end. And yet we are told by the advocates of this unscriptural doctrine that this is a just distribution of rewards and punishments under the government of God who 'is Love,' but above all, THE FATHER.

"Look at the case of one Ward, who, in one of our counties a while ago, murdered his wife—was sentenced to death, and attended by his 'Orthodox' spiritual advisers before execution. He also repented (?) and took the benefit of this Spiritual Bankrupt Act. When he stood upon the gallows, he said, he 'had but two steps to take—one into eternity and the other into glory.' And his poor wife—what became of her? Gone, 'with all her imperfections' to suffer unmitigated misery as long as God himself shall endure, and this, too, according to the unscriptural doctrine of the same churches which teach 'no change after death.' Again we ask, what can be the moral influence of such teaching?

"The truth is the burden of the most of the teaching of the day is, to 'die right;' 'make your peace with God in time,' and 'get religion before you die;' thus making religion to mainly consist in one general scramble to get into heaven and keep out of hell."

As Freethinkers, we boldly impeach the Christian plan of salvation as being essentially immoral in its tendency,—as offering a premium on vice and crime; and for doing this on previous occasions and designating it a "bankrupt scheme," the writer of this has been the subject of severe and indignant animadversion from his intimate Christian friends. Yet here is a Christian minister who takes substantially the same position as ourselves in reference to the plan of salvation as preached by Methodists and others, and denounces it as a "Spiritual Bankrupt Act." And I have made the above extracts from his pen to strengthen my position against Mr. Wendling, viz., that a belief in God and the Bible is *not* essential to social and commercial morality, and the safety of the State.

On this subject, Lord Bacon, himself a Christian, says:—

"Atheism leaves a man to sense, to philosophy, to natural piety, to laws, to reputation: all which may be guides to an outward moral virtue, though religion were not. But superstition dismounts all these, and createth an absolute monarchy in the minds of men; therefore Atheism did never perturb States, for it makes men wary of themselves, as looking no further, and we see the limes inclined to Atheism (as the time of Augustus Caesar) were civil times; but superstition, that bone of contention of many States, bringeth in a new *primum mobile* that ravishes all the spheres of government."

There are thousands of Atheists in almost every civilized country, and how is it, if Atheism tends to crime, that you will seldom or never find one in prison for any crime? Buddhism, one of the most ancient religions, long ante-dating Christianity, is essentially Atheistic. It has had, and has now, hundreds of millions of followers, and for pure morality no system of religion has ever equalled it. Webster, the Christian lexicographer, admits that Buddhism was "characterized by admirable humanity and morality.' The religion of Confucius—of him who taught the "golden rule" five centuries before Christianity appeared—was also Atheistic. Therefore, wha we "most need" is, not a "conviction that there *is* a personal God" (we hav that already; all the murderers, thieves and defaulters believe that doctrine), but we need more of the "admirable morality" of Buddhism, and more of the practice of the "golden rule" of Confucius to "do not unto others wha you would not they should do to you." As Emerson has said, "We wan some good Paganism."

Mr. Wendling's next argument for the existence of a personal God is th assumed universality of the belief in God, "among every people in every quarter of the habitable globe," now and "from the very furthest reach of history." As the value of this argument turns simply on a question of fact, and as every educated or well-read man knows that the facts in this case are against Mr. Wendling, and that his assertion is historically incorrect, it is hardly worth while to spend much time over it. However, as some readers may not have looked into the authorities on the subject, I may, perhaps not unprofitably quote briefly from some of them, and simply refer the reader to others.

To say nothing of the *Atheistic* character of the Buddhistic religion, already referred to, with its millions of followers, there have been, and are to-day, tribes and peoples who have no belief whatever in, or conception of, a God or Gods. This fact is conclusively proved by such authorities as Livingston, the great African explorer (himself a Christian), Sir John Lubbock, J. S. Mill, Darwin, and even John Wesley, the founder of Methodism, who, surely, ought to be good authority with Christians; and him we will first put in the witness box against Mr.-Wendling. Wesley says, in his Sermons, vol. 2, Sermon C:

"After all that has been so plausibly written concerning the 'innate idea of God;' after all that has been said of its being common to all men, in all ages and nations, it does not appear that man has any more idea of God than any of the beasts of the field; he has no knowledge of God at all. Whatever change may afterward be wrought by his own reflection or education, he is by nature a mere Atheist."

Charles Darwin, the greatest naturalist in the world, and who is proverbially careful in his statements, has the following on this subject in his "Descent of Man," vol. 1, p. 62-3:—

"There is ample evidence, derived not from hasty travellers, but from men who have long resided with savages, that numerous races have existed nd still exist, who have no idea of one or more Gods, and who have no vords in their languages to express such an idea."

Again, in vol. 2, p. 377, Darwin says:—

"The belief in God has often been advanced as not only the greatest, but the most complete, of all the distinctions between man and the lower nimals. It is, however, impossible, as we have seen, to maintain that this elief is innate or instinctive in man. On the other hand, a belief in all-ervading spiritual agencies seems to be universal; and apparently follows om a considerable advance in the reasoning powers of man, and from a till greater advance in his faculties of imagination, curiosity and wonder. I am aware that the assumed instinctive belief in God has been used by many persons as an argument for His existence. But this is a rash argument, as we should thus be compelled to believe in the existence of many cruel and malignant spirits, possessing only a little more power than man; for the belief in them is far more general than of a beneficent Deity. The idea of a universal and beneficent Creator of the universe does not seem to arise in the mind of man, until he has been elevated by long-continued culture."

I would refer the reader who wishes to pursue the subject further, to Livingston's writings, to Sir J. Lubbock's "Prehistoric Times," and his "Origin of Civilization," and also to the *Anthropological Review* for August, 1864.

Mr. Wendling's next argument to prove the existence of a personal God is the once celebrated but now obsolete "design" argument of Catwell and Paley; but he seems either not to know or he ignores the fact that this "design argument" has been so thoroughly refuted by the sternest logic and most indisputable natural facts that the more advanced theologians of the present day have wholly abandoned it. To reproduce these, or to give any elaborate refutation, it is unnecessary here. The whole matter may be disposed of briefly by one or two simple syllogisms which everybody can comprehend. The famous "design argument," then, may be formulated into simple syllogistic propositions thus:—

Whatever manifests design must have had a designer:

The world manifests design;

Therefore, the world must have had a designer.

This is the whole Christian reasoning on the subject in a nutshell, and it has been considered by them perfectly conclusive and unanswerable. The logic is certainly unexceptionable, that is, the conclusion is quite legitimate from the premises; but it so happens that the premises are unsound, and in such a case the most unexceptionable logic goes for naught. If premises be erroneous, though the reasoning be ever so good, the conclusion must be erroneous. The major premiss of the foregoing syllogism, that "whatever manifests design must have had a designer," is a pure assumption, if by design is meant adaptation in Nature. So, likewise, is the minor premiss an assumption if by design is meant anything more than the adaptation pervading the universe, or at least that part cognizable to us. That the *fitness and adaptation* observable in Nature do not establish intelligent design, is amply shown by the highest authorities—by the most eminent naturalists (Hæckel, Darwin, &c.) of the present day, to whom the reader is referred, and I need not here amplify in that direction. Nor is it at all necessary for my present purpose and work. It is only necessary to apply the *teductio ad absurdum* to the above argument from design to show its utter fallacy. We will admit the premises and carry the reasoning of our Christian friends out a little further. By granting the truth of their major proposition and reasoning, logically from it we can prove more than is wholesome for the theologian, as thus:—

...Whatever manifests design must have had a designer:

God, in his alleged personality and attributes, manifests design;

Therefore, God must have had a designer.

It will thus be seen that Mr. Wendling's design argument from Catwell and Paley proves entirely too much for his own good, and hence it is that the astute theologians of the day have abandoned Paley and his design argument to their fate, where they have been duly relegated by the incisive logic of the modern materialist.

Finally, Mr. Wendling comes to the moral argument, and in *conscience* finds proof of the existence of a personal God. He complacently avers that "God made man with this omnipresent 'I ought' implanted in his nature." Now, in the first place, it is a great mistake that this "I ought" or conscience is *universally* implanted in man—is "omnipresent," as Mr. Wendling puts it. That there are tribes without the moral sense of conscience, is sustained by the same unimpeachable authorities referred to in proof of the absence in them of any theistic conception or belief; and even in civilized (?) society we unfortunately find an occasional specimen of the *genus homo* with no noticeable trace of that "variable quality" we call conscience.

That conscience is *innate* in man, and a God-given faculty, instead of acquired by development, is another convenient assumption without any substantial foundation. If conscience is a Divine gift to humanity, how is it that consciences differ so widely, not only in *degree*, but in *kind*? If conscience is a Divine "monitor" and "guide" from heaven, why is it that it so often becomes a very blind guide, and leads people into many by-paths? How is it that under the sanction of conscience the most horrid crimes and cruelties against humanity have been committed in the name of God, its alleged author? How is it, if conscience is an "unerring guide" to conduct, implanted by God, that it has guided man, in the name of its author, to let out the life blood of his fellow-creatures in rivers, on account of differences of opinion *conscientiously* entertained? Does God give one man one sort of conscience and another man another and wholly different sort, leading them in opposite directions, and then prompt the conscience of one to put the other (his fellow) to death for conscience sake and for God's sake? If so, it is very questionable work, surely, for a good (?) God to be engaged in! If God implants the conscience in man, why not be fair and just and give *all* men consciences? and give them all the same article? and not give one man a tolerably good article of conscience (the Freethinker, for example) and then go and give others (some of our Christian friends, for example) so poor an article, so to speak—so flexible and elastic—that it allows them to murder, cheat, lie, slander, rob widows and orphans, and run away with other people's money and other men's wives without compunction—without any troublesome pangs from this universal "I ought" over which Mr. Wendling grows so eloquent!

The Christian world has been quite long enough teaching an irrational and absurd doctrine about conscience. They not only blunder as to its origin, but as to its nature and functions. Nearly every Christian writer defines conscience as an "inward monitor" to tell us right from wrong; a divine faculty enabling us to "*judge* between the good and the bad;" a "*guide* to conduct," &c, &c. In the light of our present mental science this definition of conscience is utterly false. Conscience is not an *intelligent* faculty at all—it is simply a feeling. By modern metaphysics conscience has been relegated from the domain of the intellect to its proper place among the emotions. Hence it *decides* nothing, *judges* nothing as between right and wrong, or anything else, for that is a function of intellect. Conscience, instead of being a "guide" or "judge," is but a blind impulse needing itself to be guided. It is simply a feeling for the right—a thirsting for the good—but the *intellect* must decide what *is* right; and the nature and character of its decisions will depend upon various circumstances, such as organization, education, &c.; and the decisions of different individuals as to right and wrong will differ as those circumstances differ. We hear a great deal about "enlightening the conscience;" but it cannot be done. You might as well talk of enlightening a sunflower, which instinctively turns its head to the light; or a vine, which instinctively creeps up the portico. The intellect, however, may be enlightened. Reason, which is the only and ultimate arbiter and guide to conduct, may be enlightened; and we may thus modify, guide and direct the blind impulses of conscience. The truth is, conscience in man, such as it is, is a development—is acquired rather than innate; has been developed by Nature instead of "implanted" by God. The moral sense, without doubt, gradually developed in man as he rose in the scale of intelligence. Where there is little or no intelligence, the moral sense would be inapplicable and incongruous, and is not needed, hence does not exist. When it is required, Nature, in perfect keeping with all her other adaptations, develops it. Darwin, in the "Descent of Man," vol. i, pp. 68-9, says:—

"The following proposition seems to me in a high degree probable—namely, that any animal whatever, endowed with well-marked social instincts, would inevitably acquire a moral sense or conscience, as soon as its intellectual powers had become as well developed, or nearly as well developed, as in man."

On this point John Stuart Mill also has the following in his "Utilitarianism," p. 45:—

"If, as is my own belief, the moral feelings are not innate, but acquired, they are not for that reason less natural."

The reader is also referred to "Psychological Inquiries," by Sir B. Brodie, for further evidence on this subject.

The moral sense, therefore, which exists in a portion of mankind—distinct traces of which are also found in some of the lower animals—has been gradually acquired during the evolution of man from a lower to a higher condition. It has come down to us from primitive barbarism through long ages of hereditary transmission. The "spiritual yearnings" of man's nature, thought by Christians to prove a God as their author, have, in like manner, been gradually acquired. These subjective emotions and desires—whether you call them *carnal* or *spiritual*—are, unquestionably, in the light of modern science, all matters of gradual development, hereditary inheritance, and education. The great doctrine of EVOLUTION in nature explains them all.

Having thus dealt with the arguments of Mr. Wendling in evidence of a personal God—a primary assumption upon which he predicates many other assumptions—there is little else in his "Reply to Robert Ingersoll" demanding attention. One or two, however, of his extraordinary assertions, it may not be amiss to look into a little; especially as Mr. Wendling, having waxed valiant over the supposed conclusiveness of his arguments, triumphantly throws down the glove to "infidelity" in this wise:—

"To my mind the great central thought of Christianity is that every living soul, of every race, of every clime, of every creed, of every condition, of every color—every living soul is worthy the Kingdom * * * And here I challenge infidelity. I lay the challenge broadly down. I challenge infidelity to name an era or a school in which this doctrine was taught prior to the advent of the Ideal Man."

Here, again, Mr. Wendling's orthodoxy is badly out of joint, and his facts at loose ends. This "central thought" that "every living soul is worthy the Kingdom" has no place in Christianity. It is by no means biblical doctrine, however well so humane an idea may fit into Mr. W.'s own mind. Hence, to designate the *brotherhood of man* the "great central thought of Christianity"—a system which is to consign a majority of mankind to an endless hell of fire and brimstone—is purely gratuitous. To claim benevolent fatherhood or brotherhood for a religion which declares that the road to hell is "broad," and many shall go in thereat, while the way to Heaven is "narrow," and few shall go in thereat, is to play fast and loose with the Bible. To say that "every soul is worthy the Kingdom," and call this the "great central thought of Christianity," in the face of what the "Word of God" cheerfully tells us on this subject, is, indeed, a "marvellous flexibility of language," which I do not at all propose to tolerate in discussion with "a lawyer," "a politician," "a man of the world," or any other man. Hear ye! O! non-elect, what comforting things the Scripture saith to you on your "future prospects!"

"For whom he did foreknow, he also did predestinate." "For the children being not yet born, neither having done any good or evil, that the purpose of God according to election might stand, not of works, but of him that calleth." "Therefore hath he mercy on whom he will have mercy, and whom he will he hardeneth." (Romans, 8th and 9th Chapters.) "The wicked are estranged from the womb; they go astray as soon as they be born, speaking lies." (Psalm 58.) "Ye believe not because ye are not of my sheep." (John 10.) "Ye be reprobates." (II. Corinth. 13.) "Jacob have I loved, but Esau have I hated." (Romans 9.) He hardened their hearts, "That seeing they may see, and not perceive; and hearing they may hear, and not understand." (Mark

4.) "Hath not the potter power over the clay." &c. (Romans 9.) "He that believeth not shall be damned."

This is benevolent (?) fatherhood, and the spirit of the *brotherhood of humanity*, with a vengance! We are distinctly told that God, "from the beginning," has deliberately fixed upon the ultimate misery and destruction of a portion of His hapless creatures; that He moulds them as clay in the hands of the potter; hardens their hearts and blinds their eyes, and then tells them He will damn them for not doing what He has prevented them from doing, and what He knows, beforehand, they cannot and will not do! This is what Mr. Wendling calls the "great central thought of Christianity—that 'every soul is worthy the Kingdom,'"—and he calls loudly upon "infidelity" to name an era or a school in which this doctrine was taught before the "Ideal Man" taught it. He is right! We cannot do it! We may search the philosophies and sacred writings of the Pagans in vain for so fiendish a doctrine. For pure, unadulterated malevolence, the Vedas, the Shaster, the Zend-Avesta, afford no parallel for this truly Christian doctrine.

If, however, Mr. Wendling challenges us to name an era or school in which the *brotherhood of man* (as we understand it) was taught before the time of the "Ideal Man," we unhesitatingly accept his challenge. It was taught by Buddha, Confucius, and numerous Pagan writers and philosophers long before the time of Jesus, for proof of which I refer the reader to Prof. Max Muller, Sir Wm. Jones, Lord, Amberly, &c, or to the writings themselves. Mr. Wendling desires us to "Tell me (him) why it is that all the creeds of Christendom and all the civilized nations unite in accepting the Ideal Man of Christianity despite the laws of climate and of race?"

I will answer this question in the Irishman's fashion, by asking one or two others. Tell me why it is, if Christianity is a divine system, and its author omnipotent, that, after eighteen centuries of active propagandism and aggression, compassing sea and land to make proselytes, it has to-day, according to recent statistics, but the meagre following of 399,200,000; while Buddhism has 405,600,000, and Brahmanism, Mohammedanism, etc., 500,000,000? Not nearly one-third of the world's population Christians, and the number rapidly diminishing! Tell me why it is, if Christianity is true that its foundations are melting down like wax in the light of Modern Science?' Tell me why it is, if the Bible is an inspired book, a divine revelation, that scarcely a single really eminent scientist or scholar of the present day accepts it as such? Tell me why it is that Atheism, Agnosticism, and Rationalism are making such rapid headway among the educated and intelligent, in every civilized country, both in the church and out of it? That the dogmas upon which Christianity rests are doomed; and as Froude, the historian, says, "Doctrines once fixed as a rock are now fluid as water?"* If the Bible can bear the light of science and historical research, how is it that these have already irrevocably sapped its very foundations; and that, as a consequence, the world is completely "honey-combed with infidelity," as a Toronto paper recently asserted of that city? The only answer Mr. Wendling can give to these questions is this: Because Christianity is unable to show its titles; because the Bible, being human in its origin, and, as a consequence, abounding in errors, both in science and morals, cannot bear the penetrating light of modern science and criticism.

* *"Science and Theology, Ancient and Modern."—The International Religio-Science Series.—Rose-Belford Publishing Company, Toronto.*

REPLY TO LYNCH

A CRUSHING (?) EDICT FROM ST. MICHAEL'S PALACE.

(*Brutem Fulmen,*) BY "Yours in Christ, (Signed), John Joseph Lynch."

Since Ingersoll's visit to Canada, Archbishop Lynch, of Toronto,-has also felt called upon to issue a bull against the Freethinkers; and, I propose to take this "bull" by the horns and *lynch* him (I may say *sub rosa* that the Bulls of Rome were long ago emasculated, yet, strangely enough, they still keep *multiplying*!) Under the circumstances, I think such a work (lynching the bull) will not be one wholly of *supererogation,*—though it may be more than a *venial* offence—indeed possibly a *mortal* sin for which I can get no *absolution*—to presume to criticise an Archbishop, and break a lance with his holy bull! I have, however, desperately resolved to take my chances of purgatory or limbo and go in for the bull.

Some of the Archbishop's flock, it would seem, had ventured to exercise the natural rights of man to the very modest extent of going to hear Mr. Ingersoll lecture, and also attending some of the meetings of the Toronto *Liberal Association*. Hence the fulmination of the aforesaid "bull," wherein his Grace, with that meekness, charity and toleration born of piety and infallibility, orders his people to "avoid all contact with these Freethinkers, their lectures and their writings," and threatens all Catholics who "go to the meetings and lectures of the Freethinkers or Atheists" with refusal of "absolution," which priestly function, he patronizingly tells them, he "reserves" to himself.

Now, may we not indulge the hope, in this age of reason, and land of at least professed liberty, and esoteric freedom of conscience, that every man, be he Catholic or Protestant, will look upon this attempted exercise of medieval bigotry and intolerance with practical disregard, and deserved contempt. As for the Freethinkers, they can afford to smile at the impotent Archbishop, who seems to imagine himself in the ninth instead of the nineteenth century, and in Rome or Spain instead of the Dominion of Canada. They can but look at him and his foolish "bull" as most ridiculous anachronisms. On reading this precious document it is plain that all this deputy "Vicegerent of God" requires to make him a first-class modern Torquemada is the power—the outward authority to carry out his subjective hatred of "brutalized" Freethinkers. But this, thanks to science, and consequent civilization, he has not got. The Rationalist can, therefore, at this day, afford to deride the malevolent, though fortunately impotent, ravings of this zealous bishop of an emasculated Church. He and his Church (the whole Christian Church) are, fortunately for humanity, shorn of their wonted strength, which, in the past, they have used with such fiendish ferocity and brutality on human kind. The day has gone by when the Church may light an *auto-da-fé* around the body of a Bruno. The time has passed when she may thrust a Galileo into prison and force him to recant the sublime truths of Astronomy. She can no longer cast a Roger Bacon into a noisome dungeon because of his scientific investigations. True, she can still, if she choose, excommunicate a Copernicus for what she denounced as his "false Pythagorean doctrine," but that is all. Darwin, Huxley, Tyndall, Proctor and the rest are safe. This relentless enemy of Science and liberty, and consequently of mankind, can no longer clutch every young science by the throat and strangle struggling truth, which, crushed to earth has risen again in its might; and history will scarcely repeat itself in the case of Bruno the Atheist, or Galileo the Astronomer, or Roger Bacon the Philosopher, or a thousand other victims of this ruthless "Bourbon of the world of thought"—the Church. She may still continue to fulminate her absurd and innocuous *anathemas*, but this is about all. The Holy Inquisition, with its two hundred and fifty thousand human victims; the Crusades with its five millions; the massacre of St. Bartholomew with its fifty thousand; to say nothing of the religious horrors of the Netherlands, of England, Scotland, and Ireland since the reformation—all these holy horrors, let us hope, are "hideous blots on the history of the past never to be repeated." Or will it be said of the future history of Christianity, as has been frankly admitted of its past by one of its ardent disciples, Baxter, that "Blood, blood, blood stains every page?"

The tables are now turning. The Church, to-day, instead of burning unbelievers, and strangling science by immuring in dungeons its votaries, is herself being strangled by science (with no loss of human blood, however). Her cruel theology and irrational dogmas are prostrate, writhing in their death throes, at the feet of the Hercules of modern science and criticism.

A little digression will not be out of order here. Our comic caricaturist at Toronto (of which, on the whole, Canada may feel proud), recently had a cartoon representing the theological Gamaliel of St. Michael's Palace, Toronto, strangling the *serpent* "Freethought." Now, though usually on the side of truth and impartiality, *Grip* has undoubtedly, in this case, taken an oblique squint at truth and justice, and has for once, at least, got the cart before the horse. Facts and truth demand that the positions of the gladiators in his cartoon must be reversed, and the zoological nomenclature corrected.

And if *Grip* had read Huxley and Tyndall, and correctly observed the signs of the times, he would scarcely have fallen into this unpardonable error. Let us quote Prof. Huxley on this subject of strangling serpents:—

"It is true that, if philosophers have suffered, their cause has been amply revenged. *Extinguished theologians lie about the cradle of every science as the strangled snakes beside that of Hercules;* and history records that, whenever science and orthodoxy have been fairly opposed, the latter has been forced to retire from the lists, bleeding and crushed, if not annihilated; scotched, if not slain. But orthodoxy is the Bourbon of the world of thought. It learns not, neither can it forget; and, though at present bewildered and afraid to move, it is as willing as ever to insist that the first chapter of Genesis contains the beginning and the end of sound science; and to visit, with such petty thunderbolts as its half-paralyzed hands can hurl those who refuse to degrade Nature to the level of primitive Judaism."—*Lay Sermons*, p. 277-8.

From this, *Grip* will see that instead of the fair form of reason and Freethought (which he represents as a snake) being strangled by a prelate of the church, it is the serpent, orthodoxy, which is being strangled by the Hercules of science. It is to be regretted that *Grip*, notwithstanding his professions of independence and impartiality, is himself obnoxious to the very moral cowardice he has so often fearlessly and justly exposed in others. Else why does he represent Freethought as a snake? Is it because Freethought is yet comparatively weak in numbers, and unpopular, and because this sort of thing will please the Church, which *is* popular and powerful? What characteristic of the snake attaches to Freethought or Freethinkers? None; and we fearlessly challenge *Grip* and the Church on this point. Freethought has none of the reptilian qualities of hypocrisy, cunning or deceit, but is frank and fearless. Amid all the obloquy, denunciation, persecution, social ostracism, calumny, and "holy bulls" hurled at them, Freethinkers have the courage of their opinions; and bear all these, as well as business detriment, for the sake of what they sacredly regard as *truth*.

What does Prof. Tyndall say of Freethinkers and Atheists? To Archbishop Lynch, who, in his pronunciamiento, says, "A person who, disbelieves in the Ten Commandments, in hell or in Heaven, can hardly be trusted in the concerns of life;" and to *Grip* who cowardly crystalizes this base assertion into a baser cartoon, I quote with pride the language of this noble man, and eminent scholar and scientist. In the *Fortnightly Review* for November, 1877, Prof. Tyndall says:

"It may comfort some to know that there are amongst us many whom the gladiators of the pulpit would call Atheists and Materialists, whose lives, nevertheless, as tested by any accessible standard of morality, would contrast more than favorably with the lives of those who seek to stamp them with this offensive brand. When I say 'offensive' I refer simply to the intention of those who use such terms, and not because Atheism or Materialism, when compared with many of the notions ventilated in the columns of religious newspapers, has any particular offensiveness to me. If I wished to find men who are scrupulous in their adherence to engagements, whose words are their bond, and to whom moral shiftiness of any kind is subjectively unknown; if I wanted a loving father, a faithful husband, an honorable neighbor, and a just citizen, I would seek him among the band of Atheists to which I refer. I have known some of the most pronounced amongst them, not only in life, but in death—seen them approaching with open eyes the inexorable goal, with no dread of a 'hangman's whip,' with no hope of a heavenly crown, and still as mindful of their duties, and as faithful in the discharge of them, as if their eternal future depended on their latest deeds."

Let the Archbishop, and *Grip*, and every reader ponder these brave words of so high an authority in defence of the reprobated class-stigmatised as "infidels," to which they refer; and then, for corroboration, compare the testimony given with the living facts around them..

The Archbishop says, these "foolish men" (the Freethinkers) are "striving to replunge the world into the depths of Barbarism and Paganism," etc., etc. To those who know that the present attitude of all the great scientists and eminent *savans* towards the dogmas of the Christian Church, is one of undoubted unbelief and hostility; and who are conversant with the history of the Archbishop's own church in particular, during the past fifteen centuries,—to them the Archbishop's vituperation is as foolish as it is ridiculous. From the days of Constantine to this year, 1880, the Church, of which this learned (?) prelate is a representative, has strenuously opposed learning, and retarded civilization; has tolerated no freedom of conscience or liberty of thought, thus narrowing instead of extending the liberty enjoyed in Pagan and Imperial Rome, over whose ruins she reared her tyrannical head. Talk of "Paganism!" His Church needs, as Emerson puts it, "some good Paganism." She left behind her the liberty even of Pagan Rome, her maligned precursor. Renan tells us, "We may search in vain, the Roman law before Constantine, for a single passage against freedom of thought, and the history of the imperial government furnishes no instance of a prosecution for entertaining an abstract doctrine." And, Mosheim, the ecclesiastical historian, tells us that the Romans exercised this toleration in the amplest manner.

"The prosecutions of the Christians by the Pagans, it is now universally conceded by Christian historians, have been greatly exaggerated; Christians have killed, in one day, for their faith nearly half as many heretics as all the Christians put to death by the Pagans during the whole period of the Pagan Empire." (The Influence of Christianity on Civilization, pp. 24-5, Underwood.)

The Archbishop's Church is, therefore, no improvement in respect of liberty or toleration, on the Paganism he reviles.

What progress the world has made in liberty and civilization, has been made, not with the assistance of the Christian Church, but in spite of its determined opposition and deadly hostility. Dr. Draper, author of the "History of the Conflict between Religion and Science," and other works, tells us that:

"Latin Christianity is responsible for the condition and progress of Europe from the fourth to the sixteenth century," and subsequently avers, "Whoever will, in in a spirit of impartiality, examine what had been done by Catholicism for the intellectual and material advancement of Europe, during her long reign, and what has been done by science in its brief period of action, can, I am persuaded, come to no other conclusion than this, that, in instituting a comparison, he has established a contrast." ("Conflict," p. 321.) Lecky, in his "History of Morals," vol. 2, p. 18, tells us:—"For more than three centuries the decadence of theological influence has been one of the most invariable signs and measures of our progress. In medicine, physical science, commercial interests, politics, and even ethics, the reformer has been confronted with theological affirmations that have barred his way, which were all defended as of vital importance, and were all compelled to yield before the secularizing influence of civilization." (Protestant as well as Catholic Christianity is, however, obnoxious to this stricture of Lecky.)

The Freethinkers "striving to replunge the world into the depths of barbarism!" What can the Archbishop's idea of barbarism be? Doubtless in his priestly mind everything is "barbarism" which does not square with the Encyclical, or with the dogmas of his infallible Church. If, however, barbarism is in reality just the opposite of our most enlightened and highest civilization in Art, Science, Literature and Ethics, it will, I have the presumption to think, be found that those "foolish men"—those "brutalized" Freethinkers—are leading the van of progress forward to a higher civilization, instead of dragging it backward to barbarism. The truth of this is patent everywhere, in every civilized country, and many of our Christian opponents admit it, though Archbishop Lynch may not. A clergyman of Toronto—Rev. W. S. Rainsford, of St. James' Cathedral—(from whom the Archbishop of St. Mary's Cathedral might probably, to his advantage, take a lesson in toleration), in a sermon preached in that city,

Nov. 17th, 1878, in speaking of Freethinkers, made use of the following language, as reported in the *Globe* of the 18th:

"This sort of infidelity, that of Materialism, has its students in the laboratory and in the library. It includes men of moral lives, of earnest purposes, * * * men who uphold morality, chastity, self-denial, perseverance with as clear a voice as Christians do, but on different grounds."

Years ago the N. Y. *Independent*, a religious paper, made the following ingenuous admission:

"To the shame of the Church it must be confessed that the foremost in all our philanthropic movements, in the interpretation of the spirit of the age, in the practical application of genuine Christianity, in the reformation of abuses in high and low places, in the vindication of the rights of man, and in practically redressing his wrongs, in the intellectual and moral regeneration of the race, are the so-called infidels in our land. The Church has pusillanimously left, not only the working oar, but the very reins of salutary reform in the hands of men she denounces as inimical to Christianity, and who are practically doing, with all their might, for humanity's sake, what the Church ought to be doing for Christ's sake; and if they succeed, as succeed they will, in abolishing slavery, banishing rum, restraining licentiousness, reforming abuses and elevating the masses, then must the recoil on Christianity be disastrous. Woe, woe, woe, to Christianity when Infidels by the force of nature, or the tendency of the age, get ahead of the Church in morals, and in the practical work of Christianity. In some instances they are already far in advance. In the vindication of Truth, Righteousness, and Liberty, *they are the pioneers*, beckoning to a sluggish Church to follow in the rear."

The *Evangelist* also, made the following admission of the same facts: "Among all the earnest minded young men, who are at this moment leading in thought and action in America, we venture to say that four-fifths are skeptical of the great historical facts of Christianity. What is held as Christian doctrine by the churches claims none of their consideration, and there is among them a general distrust of the clergy, as a class, and an utter disgust with the very aspect of modern Christianity and of church worship. This scepticism is not flippant; little is said about it. It is not a peculiarity alone of radicals and fanatics; most of them are men of calm and even balance of mind, and belong to no class of ultraists. It is not worldly and selfish. Nay, the doubters lead in the bravest and most self-denying enterprises of the day."

From a Church which has always opposed the education of the people, when she had the power, and exterminated or expatriated the best intellects under her jurisdiction, this talk of Freethinkers "re-plunging the world into the depths of barbarism" comes with a very bad grace from his Grace of Toronto. By this Church the Moriscoes were driven out of Spain—100,000 of them—and this because they were the friends of progress, of art and science. Buckle, the historian, tells us:—"When they were thrust out of Spain there was no one to fill their places; arts and manufactures either degenerated or were entirely lost, ard immense regions of arable land were left uncultivated; whole districts were suddenly deserted, and down to the present day have never been repeopled." The Jews also were expelled, as they, too, were in favor of knowledge and improvement, and this was sufficient cause for their expatriation.

This relentless enemy—the Church—of all science, all progress in knowledge among the people, ruthlessly exterminated the best minds within its grasp for centuries. Darwin, in his "Descent of Man," vol. 1, p. 171-2, says:—

"During the same period the Holy Inquisition selected with extreme care the freest and boldest men in order to burn and imprison them. In Spain alone some of the best men, those who doubted and questioned—and without doubting and questioning there can be no progress—were eliminated during three centuries at the rate of a thousand a year."

Talk to us of barbarism and paganism! A church which, from the time, nearly fifteen centuries ago, when she burnt the Alexandrian Libraries and Museum—the intellectual legacies of centuries—to the present time, has never yet called off her sleuth-hounds with which she has always hunted down the sacred principles of liberty of thought and freedom of conscience! A Church which from "the beginning of that unhappy contest," as Mosheim tells us, "between faith and reason, religion and philosophy, piety and genius, which increased in succeeding ages, and is prolonged even to our times with a violence which renders it extremely difficult to be brought to a conclusion," to this day, would hold the world in barbarous ignorance if its paralyzed hand could but avail against the resistless march of knowledge and truth! Draper, in speaking of the condition of the people under Catholicity in the 14th century, thus pictures the civilizing (?) and elevating influences of that Holy Religion:—

"There was no far reaching, no persistent plan to ameliorate the physical condition of the nations. Nothing was done to favor their intellectual development, indeed, on the contrary, it was the settled policy to keep them not merely illiterate, but ignorant. Century after century passed away, and left the peasantry but little better than the cattle in the fields. * * * Pestilences were permitted to stalk forth unchecked, or at best opposed only by mummeries. Bad food, wretched clothing, inadequate shelter, were suffered to produce their result, and at the end of a thousand years the population of Europe had not doubled."

For centuries, and centuries, in the Western Empire, subsequent to the invasion of the barbarians, when the Church this Toronto prelate owes allegiance to, had absolute control, such was the dense ignorance that scarcely a layman could be found who could sign his own name. There was very little learning, and what little there was the clergy carefully and jealously confined to themselves; and as Hallam, the historian, tells us:—

"A cloud of ignorance overspread the whole face of the church, hardly broken by a few glimmering lights, who owe almost the whole of their distinction to the surrounding darkness." The same historian (Middle Ages, p. 460,) tells us:—"France reached her lowest point at the beginning of the eighth century, but England was, at that time, more respectable, and did not fall into complete degradation until the middle of the ninth. There could be nothing more deplorable than the state of Italy during the succeeding century. In almost every council the ignorance of the clergy forms a subject for reproach. It is asserted by one held in 992 that scarcely a single person was to be found in Rome itself, who knew the first elements of letters. Not one priest of a thousand in Spain, about the age of Charlemagne, could address a common letter of salutation to one another."

Lecky, in his "History of Morals," vol. 2, p. 222, tells us that:

"Mediæval Catholicity discouraged and suppressed, in every way, secular studies," and further, that, "Not till the education of Europe passed from the monasteries to the universities; not until Mahomedan science and classical freethought and industrial independence broke the sceptre of the Church, did the intellectual revival of Europe commence."

And, I would ask Archbishop Lynch, what was the condition of the Byzantine Empire during the thousand years or upwards of its existence?—An empire under the sway of his Church, from its foundation by the first Christian emperor, Constantine—that exemplary Christian murderer who, because the Pagan priests refused him absolution for his enormities, hastened to the bosom of the Christian Church, whose priests he found more pliable, having little compunction or hesitancy about granting absolution to the new proselyte. What is the record of history touching this Empire under the aegis of Catholic Christianity? The historian Lecky thus graphically sets forth its condition:—

"The universal verdict of history is that it constitutes, without a single exception, the most thoroughly base and despicable form that civilization has yet assumed. Though very cruel and very sensual, there have been times when cruelty assumed more ruthless, and sensuality more extravagant aspects, but there has been no other enduring civilization so absolutely destitute of all the forms, the elements, of greatness, and none to which the epithet *mean* may be so emphatically applied. The Byzantine Empire was pre-eminently the age of treachery. Its vices were the vices of men who ceased to be brave without learning to be virtuous. * * * The history of the empire is a monotonous story of the intrigues of priests, eunuchs and women, of poisonings, of conspiracies, of uniform ingratitude, of perpetual fratricides." In speaking of the condition of the Western Empire the same author proceeds:—"A boundless intolerance of all divergence of opinion was united with an equally boundless toleration of all falsehood and deliberate fraud, that could favor received opinions. Credulity being taught as a virtue, and all conclusions dictated by authority, a deadly torpor sank upon the human mind, which for many centuries almost suspended its action, and was only broken by the scrutinizing, innovating and free-thinking habits that accompanied the rise of the industrial republics in Italy. Few men who are not either priests or monks would not have preferred to live in the best days of the Athenian or of the Roman republics, in the age of Augustus, or in the age of the Antonines rather than in any period that elapsed between the *triumph of Christianity and the fourteenth century*."

The same historian, whose accuracy Archbishop Lynch will scarcely attempt to impeach, thus judicially and impartially sums up the influences of Catholic Christianity both in the Eastern and Western Empires during many centuries when it had the fullest sway:—

"When we remember that in the Byzantine Empire the renovating power of theology was tried in a new capital, free from Pagan traditions, and for more than one thousand years unsubdued by barbarians, and that in the west, the Church, for at least seven hundred years after the shocks of the invasion had subsided, exercised a control more absolute than any other moral or intellectual agency has ever attained, it will appear, I think, that the experiment was very sufficiently tried. It is easy to make a catalogue of the glaring vices of antiquity, and to contrast them with the pure morality of Christian writings; but, if we desire to form a just estimate of the realized improvement, we must compare the classical and ecclesiastical civilizations as wholes, and must observe in each case not only the vices that were repressed but also the degree and variety of positive excellence attained."

Before the art of printing was discovered, the Church had less difficulty in keeping the people in ignorance, but after the invention of that boon to mankind she found herself ominously confronted with the tree of life from which the people would soon learn to pluck the fruit of knowledge. Hence the establishment, by Pope Paul IV., about the middle of the sixteenth century, of the *Index Expurgatorius*, whose functions, we are told, was "to examine books and manuscripts intended for publication, and to decide whether the people may be permitted to read them." This is what his Grace of St. Michael's Palace, in Toronto, proposes to do for the good Catholics of that city—decide what they shall read and what they shall not read, as though they were ninnies and not able to decide that matter for themselves! The fact is, however, that, in this priestly arrogance and assumption, the Archbishop is consistent enough; for, although such mediæval tyranny is altogether inconsistent with the spirit of this age, and ludicrously out of place in 1880, in the City of Toronto, it, nevertheless, perfectly accords with the tenets and spirit as well as the antecedents of his Church; which, while it accuses Freethinkers of "barbarism," allows not an inch of latitude of private judgment in matters of religion, and tolerates no freedom of conscience: And what is this but barbarism? All freedom of conscience was fiercely denounced by Gregory XVI. as insane folly, and the Archbishop of Toronto reiterates this unsavory stigma on civilization. And why shouldn't he? Theology never learns. The Church changes not. How can she when she is infallible? Yet an infallible Pope of an infallible Church, not long since, found himself, while encompassed with many difficulties, spiritual and temporal, to be about like other weak mortals in flesh and blood; and, though infallible, remember, and with the power of miracles and all that, he succumbs and whiningly complains to a vulgar world that he is "a prisoner in his own palace in Rome!" And the heretical and sceptical world—the "outside barbarians"—with a contemptuous leer, gape at the queer spectacle of the "Vicegerent on Earth" of an all-powerful God being obliged so easily to succumb to heresy—to a little temporal power. Such, however, is life—or rather the "mysterious ways of providence," which "ways" always seem though, as Cromwell observed, to be on the side of the heaviest artillery,—not the artillery of heaven, but the base artillery of earth. Indeed, this worldly artillery—the artillery of science and civilization—has, in this nineteenth century, been making such havoc with creeds, confessions, and dogmas, that the crowning dogma of all—this fundamental pillar of the Vatican, the dogma of infallibility—was, it would seem, fast becoming a *dead dog*; when the Holy Catholic Church finds it imperatively incumbent upon her to attempt a resuscitation. This happened in Rome in "*anno domini*" 1870, at that great Ecumenical Council—that unique anachronism of the nineteenth century. I know not whether that mediæval assembly of Holy "Fathers in God" was honored by the presence of his Grace of St. Michael's Palace, in Toronto, or not; but, be that as it may, his reverence's entire loyalty to the notorious Encyclical and Syllabus of that Council is not to be questioned or doubted. The miniature Toronto *bull* of May 9th, 1880, has the true Vatican ring of the big *bull* of the Council in Rome in 1870. It, too, denounced, with its usual, though harmless, *anathema*, Atheism, Pantheism, Naturalism, Rationalism and every other ism that failed to square with Papal dogma. By the fulmination of that Syllabus the world learned among many other things, that "No one may interpret the Sacred Scriptures contrary to the sense in which they are interpreted by Holy Mother Church, to whom such interpretation belongs." It was further decreed that "All the Christian faithful are not only forbidden to defend, as legitimate conclusions of science, those opinions which are known to be contrary to the doctrine of faith, especially when condemned by the Church, but are rather absolutely bound to hold them for errors wearing the deceitful appearance of truth."

As examples of the holy canons which were actually fulminated and promulgated by that Ecumenical Council in the latter part of this 19th century, here are a few:—

"Who shall refuse to receive, for sacred and canonical, the books of Holy Scripture in their integrity, with all their parts, according as they were enumerated by the Holy Council of Trent, or shall deny that they are inspired by God, *Let him be anathema*."

"Who shall say that human sciences ought to be pursued in such a spirit of freedom that one may be allowed to hold as true their assertions, even when opposed to revealed doctrine, *Let him be anathema*."

"Who shall say that it may at any time come to pass, in the progress of science, that the doctrines set forth by the Church must be taken in another sense than that in which the Church has ever received and yet receives them, *Let him be anathema*."

These are the modest assumptions of the Church of Rome in this age; and a prelate of that Church breathes the same noxious vapors forth into the intellectual atmosphere of the City of Toronto! It remains to be seen whether in Toronto there are such slaves or fools as will submit to this worse than Egyptian bondage. Will intelligent Catholics put their necks in a yoke so galling? None but slaves or barbarians would do it. The Archbishop would thus fain make barbarians of his own people, and then he would have the pagans at home without hunting among Freethinkers for them. In his lecture in Napanee, in April last, Col. Ingersoll gave it as his opinion that any man—no matter what Church he belonged to, or what country he lived in—who claimed rights for himself which he denied to others, is a barbarian! Now, according to this definition, who are the barbarians? The Freethinkers, or the Archbishop himself and those he ignominiously holds in mental bondage?

In conclusion, we thank Archbishop Lynch for his timely "bull." As a propagandist document for the spread of Freethought, and really in the interests of those "foolish" and "brutalized" Freethinkers against whom it was directed, it must prove a great success. It is another illustration of the essentially bigoted and intolerant spirit of Christianity in general.*

** I am well aware that the Protestant sects of Christianity repudiate this charge of the intolerant and persecuting spirit of Christianity in general, and vainly attempt to shift the whole onus and odium upon the Church of Rome. They tell us that Christianity itself is not persecuting—that it is not responsible for having reddened the earth with blood—but that this was all done contrary to the spirit and teachings of Christianity by men who were not really Christians. We deny it. We take the position that Christianity itself is essentially intolerant and persecuting in spirit; and, we take the New Testament itself to prove it. We take Christ's alleged words as reported there, and Paul's alleged words as reported there, and can thereby abundantly sustain our charge. "He that believeth not shall be damned." "A man that is a heretic after the first and second admonition, reject." What is that but the quintessence of bigotry and intolerance? "I would they were even cut off which trouble you." How kind! "Think not that I come to send peace on earth, etc., etc" Scores of passages could be quoted from the New Testament of similar import, and the Old Testament is worse yet, for it recommends putting even your wives or brothers to death should they try to persuade you to worship their God.—See Deut. 13, 6, 7 and 8.*

REPLY TO "BYSTANDER"

I approach this part of my prescribed duty with some hesitation, and not a little reluctance. *Bystander* is brilliant, learned, independent, and honest; and for these qualities, though differing from him on some important subjects, I entertain a respect and esteem amounting to affection. I hope, therefore, that I may not write a word here having even the semblance of discourtesy; for of that sort of treatment the gentleman in question has had a full share since he honored Canadians by casting his lot amongst us.

For the benefit of some readers who, possibly, may not have seen it, I may say that *The Bystander* is a "Monthly Review of Current Events," published in Toronto by Messrs. Hunter, Rose & Co., and written by a certain distinguished literary gentleman, as referred to above, whose name I would like to give here only that I feel in courtesy bound to respect the "impersonality of journalism," the protection of which the gentleman in question has the right, and with good reason, to claim.

The last three issues of *The Bystander* (for April, May and June) have each a paper on Col. Ingersoll, his lectures, and cognate subjects; the general tone of which is very liberal, but, at the same time, containing strictures upon Mr. Ingersoll and his teachings which I consider unfair and unjust (unintentionally no doubt), and to which I here propose briefly to reply.

Having heard Mr. Ingersoll lecture but once I am not in a position from personal knowledge to speak fully as to the alleged "blasphemy," and his general "tone" on the platform; but this much I can say, that *Bystander's* assertion that "he" (Ingersoll) "repels all decent men, whatever their convictions; for no decent man likes blasphemy any more than he likes obscenity," is certainly not true of the one lecture I heard, or of the score of others of his I have read. I humbly claim to be myself a "decent man," and I did not find myself "repelled" on listening to Ingersoll's lecture, but rather attracted. I also saw many decent people at the lecture (some from a distance), and they did not seem repelled; but, like myself, well-pleased. In Toronto, according to the reports in the *Evening Telegram,* there were large audiences of decent, intelligent people: and instead of being repelled, they greeted the lecturer with the most enthusiastic approbation and applause, repeated over and over again. The same reception was accorded him in Montreal, Belleville and Napanee.

Bystander contrasts Ingersoll's "offensive tone" on the platform with the "gentleness and sympathy of the Christian preacher on Mars' Hill," who, he tells us, "delivered the truths he bore at once with the dignity of simple earnestness, and with perfect tenderness towards the beliefs which he came to supersede." Let us, for a moment, examine this claim of "simple earnestness," and "perfect tenderness" in behalf of Paul the great preacher of the New Testament. Paul says, (Roman iii. 7) "For if the truth of God hath more abounded through my lie unto his glory, why yet am I also judged as a sinner?" He also tells us (2nd Cor. 12: 16) that "being *crafty,* I caught you with guile," and likewise assures us that he was "all things to all men;" to the Jews he "became as a Jew," etc. What "simple earnestness" this is truly! And the Church of Christ has nearly always acted in accordance with this Scriptural doctrine that in *lying* for God's sake the "end justifies the means." Mosheim, the ecclesiastical historian, tells us that in the early ages of the Christian Church, "It was an act of virtue to deceive and lie, when by that means the interest of the church might be promoted."

As to Paul's "perfect tenderness toward the beliefs which he came to supersede," let us look a little into that. In writing to the Galatians he says [tenderly] "As we said before, so say I now again, if any man preach any other gospel unto you than that you have received, let him be *accursed.*" (Gal. 1:9.) That is tender toleration for you! Again, "A man that is a heretic after the first and second admonition, reject" (Titus 4:9.) "I would they were even cut off which trouble you" (Gal. 5: 12.) We, Freethinkers, would stand a poor chance to-day if Paul's precepts were carried out! Again, "If any man love not the Lord Jesus Christ, let him be *Anathema Maranatha*" (1 Cor. 16: 22.)-What "perfect tenderness" this is! With a vengeance are these curses and maledictions tender! *Bystander* may search in vain in Ingersoll's lectures, or any Freethinkers' writings, for such consummate bigotry, intolerance, and even cruelty as this "Christian preacher" pours out upon all who venture to differ from him in belief. And what "perfect tenderness" in Paul to denounce and stigmatize even those of his own church—his co-religionists—as *"false apostles, deceitful workers, dogs, and liars!"* Did *Bystander* or anybody else ever hear such language from Ingersoll or any other Freethinker? Is it not "offensive to any sensible and right-minded man?" Does it not "repel all decent men?"

Bystander admits that when Ingersoll "attacks dogmatic orthodoxy he is in the right." What more does he attack? This is exactly what he does attack, and *Bystander* admits that in so doing he is doing right, thus showing that he himself does not believe in dogmatic orthodoxy. Now, if the Christian's God, as described in the Bible, is included in "dogmatic orthodoxy" (and He surely must be) is Ingersoll blasphemous in attacking Him? Surely not, according to *Bystander* himself. *Bystander* may say, however, that he does not mean to include the Christian's God in the "irrational and obsolete orthodoxy," against which he admits "Ingersoll's arguments are really telling." But does *Bystander* himself believe in the God of the Bible? From the tenor of his language he surely cannot. Does he believe in the God of whom the Bible itself gives the following description? (For want of time to refer to, and space to insert chapter and verse, they are not given, but every Bible reader will recognize the passages given as substantially correct):—

"He burns with anger; his lips are full of indignation, and his tongue as a devouring fire." "His fury is poured out like fire, and the rocks are thrown down by him." "The Lord awaketh as one out of sleep, and like a mighty man that shouteth by reason of wine." "Smoke came out of his nostrils, and fire out of his mouth, so that coals were kindled by it." "He had horns coming out of his hand." "Out of his mouth went a sharp two-edged sword." "The Lord shall roar from on high. He roareth from his habitation. He shall shout as they that tread the grapes." "He is a jealous God." "He stirred up jealousy." "He was jealous to fury." "He rides upon horses." "The Lord is a man of war." "His anger will be accomplished, and his fury rest upon them, and then he will be *comforted!*" "His arrows shall be drunken with blood." "He is angry with the wicked every day." "A fire is kindled in mine anger and shall burn unto the lowest hell. I will heap mischief upon them; I will spend my arrows upon them I will also send the teeth of beasts upon them, and the poison of the serpents... both the young man and the virgin, the suckling also, and the man of gray hairs." [What did the "suckling" do to merit this?] "He reserveth wrath for his enemies." "He became angry and swore." "He cried and roared."

Does *Bystander* believe in a God like that? whom it is "blasphemy," it seems, for Ingersol to attack! It is true there are good qualities and attributes ascribed to God by the Bible as well as bad; but that does not affect the fact that these are ascribed to him; while the co-existence of two diametrically opposite sets of attributes in the same Being is simply absurd. Why is it blasphemy to attack such a conception of God, any more than to attack any of the other Pagan gods of antiquity? As he is represented in the Bible, He is certainly no better than they; and *Bystander* himself would have little hesitancy in making an onslaught on the Pagan gods. When primitive Judaism and Christianity set up a God for *our* worship and adoration, and at the same time tells us, "by the book," that He commanded the cruel, fiendish, and indiscriminate murder of men, women, and innocent children, we beg to decline to worship, or adore, or believe in any such Being; and we do not think it "blasphemy" to attack the false belief and the false God. When we read in the "word of God" that the Lord commanded one of his prophets to diet on excrement; that the Lord met Moses at a tavern and tried to kill him (see Exodus, 4, 24); that the sun and moon stood still; that it rained forty days and nights, and that nearly the whole world was drowned; that the first man—Adam—was made of clay, and Eve of a rib, about 6000 years ago; that the world was made in six days, and that vegetation flourished before there was any sun,—when we read of all these wonderful things, we beg to be excused from believing them, and claim the right to ridicule them to our heart's content. If this is "disrespect," or "insult," or an "ignoble spirit of irreverence," then we plead guilty to the charge, and are willing to abide by it.

We do not deny that there may be a God; we only deny the existence of such a one as the Bible sets forth. We attack only the gods whom barbarous peoples have fashioned in their own imaginations and set up for our worship, and not any high or noble conception of a Deity. We fully admit the existence of a great and mysterious power or force in the universe which we cannot understand or comprehend. We believe with Spencer in the great *Unknown* and *Unknowable*, and have no "attack" to make upon this power, no word of ridicule, no blasphemy; but, like Tyndall, stand in its presence with reverence and awe, acknowledging our ignorance.

While, however, acknowledging this unseen Power, we decline to anthropomorphise it—to call it a *person* or *being*, and invest it with mental and moral functions similar to our own, differing only in degree not in kind. It is only the anthropomorphism we attack—only the superstitions, assumptions and dogmas. We only attack that which is incredible and absurd—that which "shocks reason." We believe in religion—the Religion of Humanity—to do right—a religion of *works* instead of faith and creeds, and *Bystander* himself admits that "religion is carrying a weight which it cannot bear," and that, "unless the credible can be separated from the incredible, the reasonable from that which shocks reason, there will be a total eclipse of faith."

"The Cosmogony of Moses," says *Bystander*, "will, of course not bear the scrutiny of modern science; few probably are now so bigoted as to maintain that it will." If it will not bear such scrutiny, is it blasphemy to attack it, or its author? for the God of the Bible is the alleged author of that Cosmogony, inspiring Moses or whoever wrote it. But *Bystander* further remarks that the Mosaic Cosmogony "need not fear comparison with the Cosmogony of any other race." We thank him for that favor. It is exactly what we claim, to wit, that the Cosmogony of Moses, like all the others, is simply a human production, for it would be absurd to talk of "comparing" an *inspired* Cosmogony of *divine origin* with *human* Cosmogonies. Hence, according to *Bystander* himself, the Mosaic Cosmogony is simply, like the rest, human: only he thinks it a little better than the others. It will not, however, "bear the scrutiny of modern science." Very likely not! What then, becomes of the "fall of man," the "redemption" the "Ideal Man," and the whole Christian Superstructure which rests upon the Mosaic Cosmogony? If the pillars are taken away the building *must* come down.

It is also admitted by *Bystander* that "The moral code of Moses is tribal and primeval; it is alien to us who live under the ethical conditions of high civilization and the Religion of Humanity." Precisely so! And for this magnificent favor also, we again thank *Bystander*. No materialist or utilitarian could have possibly put it better; albeit a Christian would experience some moral obfuscation in trying to make out why, if the "moral code of Moses" is from heaven, it should be "alien to us" and to these times? He would be hardly able to understand why he should be comparing his *Divine* code with *Pagan* codes to see whether it is "worse or better than other codes framed in the same stage of human progress?" Let the Freethinkers take courage. *Bystander*, to all appearances, will soon be squarely on our side; and then we can truthfully say, that though the Christians have the greatest scientist, probably, in Canada (Prof. Dawson, of Montreal,) on their side, we will have the greatest scholar, historian and *literateur* in Canada on *our* side. Three cheers in the Liberal camp for *Bystander!* Indeed, we have some hopes, too, even of Prof. Dawson, whose Mosaic orthodoxy seems to be relaxing a little of late; and he evidently feels his isolation, his scientific brethren all being on our side.

While writing this, the Montreal *Daily Witness* of June 15th, 1880, comes to hand from a Freethought octogenarian friend in Port Hope (Wm. Sisson, Esq.) with the familiar pencil mark, drawing my attention to a report of the proceedings of "The Congregational Union," at present in session in Montreal. From it I learn that Rev. Hugh Pedley, B. A., made an address before the *Union* on "The Freethought of the Age," from which I cull the following, as reported in the *Witness*:—

"One of the principal difficulties," he said (of the clergy), "was the prevalence of freethought among the people. There was a time when the New Testament was received by almost everybody * * * But things had changed * * * Some time ago the weapons of skilled historians were turned first against the Old and then against the New Testament * * * Dr. Norman McLeod, writing from Germany, said, 'I am informed on credible testimony that ninety-nine out of every hundred persons here are sceptics.' * * * Germany was to-day more Pagan than Christian * * * The press passed up and down the land, scattering into every home things which set men thinking." [Ah! there is the secret; when men begin to think and reason on theological subjects as they do on secular, good-bye creeds! goodbye confessions!] "Goldwin Smith, a man who had so studied the past as to be able to interpret the present, had told us that a religious collapse of the most complete and tremendous character was apparent on every hand." It was only very recently that a sceptical work on 'Supernatural Religion' passed through a number of editions in a few months. Col. Ingersoll had recently visited the country. He came, he saw, and in some sense he conquered. (Cries of No! No!) The second night he had a much larger attendance than on the first. No matter who, ran Ingersoll down, he was a man of great power of oratory and strong in those qualities which control audiences.

The Rev. gentleman then referred deprecatingly to the inadequate-college training of theological students in "apologetics," as they were not allowed to read the works of sceptics for themselves, but had to take their tutors' version of the sceptics' arguments. This "putting up a little argument and then knocking it down," he said was neither "the fair nor the true way." He recommended putting "the very sceptical works into the hands of the students, and he would even say to go and hear Ingersoll if he came."

That "man's idea of God rises with his progress in civilization," *Bystander* admits; but he attempts to explain the fact away on theistic grounds, and dilute its strength as an argument that God is simply a projection of the human mind. He asks:—

"If this conception" (a conception of God) "flows from no reality, from what does it flow? It is a phenomenon of which, as of other phenomena, there must be some explanation; and we have not yet chanced to see in the writings of any Agnostic an explanation which seemed at all satisfactory."

I would respectfully suggest to *Bystander* that there *is* a satisfactory explanation, though to him it may not be so. In answering his question I will ask another. If the conception of, or belief in, a devil or devils, flows from no reality, from what does it flow? The same of witches, fairies, sprites, hob-goblins, *et hoc genus omne*. Belief in these is quite as general as belief in God, though *Bystander's* question seems to assume that belief in the latter is universal. This, however, is not the case, as has been conclusively shown in the foregoing reply to Wend-ling. Therefore, this "conception" argument, like the famous "design" argument, proves too much, and consequently proves nothing. As to the *origin* of the belief in spiritual agencies, and conceptions of God, Darwin tells us it is not difficult to comprehend how they arose. He says, "Descent of Man," vol. i, p. 63-5:—

"As soon as the important faculties of imagination, wonder, and curiosity, together with some power of reasoning, had become partially developed, man would naturally have craved to understand what was passing around him, and have vaguely speculated on his own existence * * * The belief in spiritual agencies would easily pass into the belief of one or more Gods."

Bystander, while freely admitting that the Theistic theory is compassed with difficulties; and requires "re-statement," reminds us that the- "materialistic hypothesis is not free from difficulty." The difficulty he discovers in materialism relates to the order of priority of matter and force. He asks:—

"Which of the two is the First Principle? Force cannot have been produced by matter, for without force, matter cannot move, change, or generate at all. Matter cannot have been produced by force, because force is nothing but the impulsion of matter. Apparently there must have been something before both, which produced them and determined their relations; and it must be something beyond the range of sense."

Bystander. I think, has not correctly apprehended the materialistic position here, and hence the argument for a "something before both matter and force which produced them," being built upon a postulated premiss which we cannot accept, has no weight in establishing the existence of a God behind matter and force. His error lies in the assumption of the possibility of matter and force existing separately and independently. He asks, "Which of the two is the First Principle?" Our answer is, there can be no *first* as between matter and force, for there can be no matter without force, and *vice versa*. The two are inseparable, even in conception, and the existence of one is absolutely essential to the existence of the other. Hence the argument proceeding from the assumption of their divisibility and possible independence fails. The Theist has no right whatever, logically speaking, to assume that there "must have been something before matter and force which produced them." So long as matter and force are amply adequate (as far as we can discern) to the production of all cognizable phenomena, we are not warranted in assuming the existence of any being or thing behind them. As soon as the Theist does this, we have the logical right to carry his reasoning further, and at once assume something else behind it again, and thus not only one but a thousand gods could be postulated without the shadow of real proof of one of them.

There is an ultimate ground, however, upon which the Theist and Materialist may meet in common, and, so far as I can see, the only ultimate position they can occupy in perfect corelation. The universe exists; man as a part of the universe—a mode of existence—is here; in this we agree. Man, then, being himself the highest intelligence he knows of, continually seeks an explanation of the universe and of himself as a part of it. This is the common ground upon which we all stand—Rationalist, Theist, Agnostic, Atheist—barbarous and civilized—the weakest and the mightiest intellect.

All seek to explain the great mystery of the universe—some one way, some another—from the rude thaumaturgic fancies of the primitive barbarian up to the abstruse speculations and subtle reasonings of the cultured Pantheist, intellectual Agnostic, and logical Materialist. It is true one may be more reasonable and logical than the rest (as I undoubtedly think is the case), yet they all occupy the common ground of uncertainty. Not one can *demonstrate* his position, and in this we are all alike. (One, however, among all the rest thinks he *knows* he is *right* and can prove it, viz., the dogmatic Christian Theist.) We may all, therefore, stand together in the presence of Nature and acknowledge our ignorance. Though each school has its theory, its hypothesis, its solution, yet the mystery of the mighty universe is still an unsolved problem.

REPLY TO "A RATIONALIST"

We have another reply to Ingersoll in a pamphlet of twenty pages, issued in Toronto, with the following modest title:—"A Refutation of Col. R. G. Ingersoll's Lectures, by 'A Rationalist.'" This proemial announcement is certainly calculated to excite high expectations; but it is only necessary to look into the rational (?) "refutation" (?) to see that the names the writer has given himself and pamphlet are both misnomers. How such an irrational jumble of orthodoxy, heterodoxy, obsolete philosophy, and moribund metaphysics could by any possibility pass for rationalism, even in the eyes of its author, is one of those profound mysteries which "no fellah can understand." Is it not a little singular that all these "replies" and "refutations" from the orthodox side come from theological nondescripts—from men who are but half orthodox (the other half not being recognizable), and not one reply from a thoroughly orthodox champion? A correlative fact, not without much significance, is that, though no argument comes from the orthodox side, the denunciations all come from that source. On the other hand in proportion as the opposing champion is unorthodox, in that ratio is he tolerant, courteous, and in favor of free speech and equal rights. "A Rationalist's" essay is pervaded by the kindliest spirit personally towards his opponent, and this, in a measure, redeems its literary and logical defects.

Though "Rationalist" zealously defends the Bible, and argues for a God, it is impossible to tell how much of the Bible he accepts, or what God he believes in. He says, "every jot and tittle of the Bible is inspired," yet in another place tells us, "The Apostle Paul is not one of the inspired writers," as "His words will not bear a spiritual interpretation." It would, therefore, seem that no part of the Bible is inspired except that which will stand this method of "spiritual interpretation." To get rid of the numerous errors, absurdities, and immoralities contained in the Bible, "Rationalist" spiritualizes them. He has a first-class recondite and spiritual meaning for every one of them, which seems to be entirely satisfactory—to himself. With the utmost facility everything is explained away; and armed with his occult style of Bible exegesis he can laugh at the infidel scientist. He says we must "rub off the literal meaning" in order to get at the spiritual, and by this convenient method every difficulty between the two sacred lids vanishes into thin air. This "rubbing off" business he also applies to the God of the

Bible, whose characteristic *anthropomorphism* "Rationalist," of course, rubs all off, even his *intelligence*. So that there would seem to be little more left of the Jewish Jehovah, under modern scriptural exegesis, than what Beecher describes as a "dim and shadowy influence." "Rationalist" divests Deity of intelligence to escape the effects of the following argument:—

Intelligence presupposes a greater intelligence,

God has intelligence,

Therefore, there must be an intelligence greater than God.

Seeing the logical force of this, he quibbles thus: "We do not say that God *has* intelligence, but that God *is* wisdom in form and love in essence, and therefore the infinite source of all intelligence." This will not do, Mr. "Rationalist!" It is entirely too vague. You must either contend for a personal or an impersonal God. Give us either Deism or Pantheism, and not an incongruous mixture, and then we will know on what ground to meet you. If you mean that God is simply the aggregate, or even the essence, of all intelligence, all love, all good, why this is a mere abstraction, and even an Atheist might accept it; but if you are contending for anything like the Christian's God, as set forth in the Bible, you will have to alter your definitions very materially.

As a specimen illustration of "Rationalist's" spiritual method of resolving Scriptural difficulties I give below his version of the story of Elisha, the children, and the bears, under the "rubbing off" process. We, Freethinkers, he says, will not "object to the bears" when we understand what the story means, and here is his elucidation, *verbatim et literatim*:—

"Elisha represents the external or literal words of Holy Writ on which the mantle of spiritual truth still rests. Children represent affections—don't fond mothers even yet call them 'little loves?'—They also correspond to the opposite, and so evil loves which destroy obedience to the external life of goodness, taught in, at least, some of the literal words of Scripture, naturally mock at the baldness of Elisha. Baldness, since it refers to the head, and the head corresponds to that union of will and intellect in man which rules, and is, the life, and ultimates in the very extreme of its very minute external, corresponds to the most external of the will and thought of Elisha, who represents the literal meaning of Scripture. So this incident means that evil loves could see no ultimate good to *themselves* in the doing of any good in a practical every-day way even where that was clearly enjoined, and rendered as beautiful externally as hair is, and therefore mocked at it, or rather at what seemed to them the lack of it. Then the bears, which correspond to the animal passions of the animal man, came out of the woods—woods correspond to the natural perceptions of natural truth in man—and utterly destroyed these evil loves out of the life. Again you see we find the same truth; that the Lord implants remains of goodness and truth in every degree of man's life, even in the natural man, fitted to cope with and conquer his evils, if man himself will but permit it."

There's a sample of "spiritual interpretation" for you! And what *clearness* is there, dear reader! Just return to the fourth sentence of the above extract, commencing with "Baldness," and re-read it, and see if you can make anything out of it. What the sentence does really mean is to me as profound a mystery as the incantations of a Gypsy thaumaturgist. It would be interesting to get "Rationalist" to try his hand at spiritualizing some of the following passages of Holy Writ:—

"In the same day shall the Lord shave with a razor that is hired," &c. "And it came to pass by the way in the inn, that the Lord met him" (Moses) "and sought to kill him." "I have seen God face to face." *Per Contra*: "No man hath seen God at any time." "I am the Lord, I change not, I will not go back, neither will I repent." *Per Contra*: "And God repented of the evil that he said he would do unto them, and he did it not." "There is no respect of persons with God." *Per Contra*: "Jacob have I loved, and Esau have I hated." "I am a jealous God, visiting the iniquities of the fathers upon the children." *Per Contra*: "The son shall not bear the iniquity of the father." "It is impossible for God to lie." *Per Contra*: "If the Prophet be deceived when he hath spoken a thing, I the Lord have deceived that Prophet." "Be not afraid of them that kill the body." *Per Contra*: "And after these things Jesus would not walk in Jewry, because the Jews sought to kill him." "And the anger of the Lord was kindled against Israel, and he moved David against them to say, 'Go number Israel.'" *Per Contra*: "And Satan provoked David to number Israel." "I bear witness of myself, yet my record is true." *Per Contra*: "If I bear witness of myself, my witness is not true." "A man is not justified by the works of the law." *Per Contra*: "Ye see, then, how that by works a man is justified." "There shall no evil happen to the just." *Per Contra*: "All that will live godly in Christ Jesus shall suffer persecution." "Wisdom's ways are ways of pleasantness and all her paths are peace." *Per Contra*: "In much wisdom is much grief and he that increaseth knowledge increaseth sorrow." "It shall not be well with the wicked, neither shall he prolong his days." *Per Contra*: "Wherefore do the wicked live, become old, yea, are mighty in power." "Thou shalt not: commit adultery." *Per Contra*: "Then said the Lord unto me, 'Go get, love a woman, an adulteress.'"

Here, certainly, is ample scope for exegetical ingenuity. The passages quoted, besides scores of others, many of them too indecent for these pages, would seem to require the touch of "Rationalist's" spiritual interpretation wand. When the literal meaning is "rubbed off," the occult, spiritual meaning will appear.

As a sample of "Rationalist's" metaphysical philosophy I give the following:—

"Will and love are identical... Will or love is life. A man cannot think unless he wills to think; and he can only think that which he wills—only that and nothing more. He can only do what he wills and thinks. There is no action which is not the effect of will and its thought. A man wills in order to think," etc. He also tells us that God gave man a will "as *free* as His own." Matter is spoken of as "mere dead inert matter."

Is more evidence than this needed that "Rationalist" is living in the past, and has utterly failed to grasp modern thought? His philosophy is bad, but his metaphysics is worse. Any man who at this day attempts to "refute" Materialists should at least be somewhat acquainted with the results of modern thought and scientific research; but "Rationalist" has apparently advanced no further than the occult Swedenborgian mysticism of the last century. Further, to talk to-day of "dead inert matter," is to talk the language of an obsolete philosophy of the past; for modern science and philosophy alike agree that matter is not "that mere empty *capacity* which philosophers have pictured her to be, but the universal mother who brings forth all things as the fruit of her own womb." As Pope says:—

"See thro' this air, this ocean, and this earth, All matter quick and bursting into birth."

Equally absurd is this talk about "Free Will" and "Free Moral Agency." These metaphysico-theological dogmas have melted in the light of mental science, and are now as "dead as a door nail," of which fact "Rationalist" will be convinced if he will take the trouble to look into Hamilton, Combe, Mill, Buckle, Lewes, Spencer, Huxley and Tyndall, and he will then, probably, write no more such nonsense as quoted above. It is not necessary, however, for any observant and thoughtful man to go to any authorities outside his own mind to be convinced of the fallacy of the "Free Will" dogma, for his own observation and reflection will do it. And "Rationalist" can have the same conviction without the aid of science or philosophy,—without even observation or reflection. Let him turn to his Bible, which he champions, and read it, and he will find abundant proof (such as it is) that man's will is not free. Let him read the 8th, 9th and 11th Chapters of Romans. Let him then read Phil. 2, 13, "For it is God which worketh in you *both to will and to do* of His good *pleasure*." Then read Isaiah, 46, 910, "I am God and there is none like me, *declaring the end from the beginnings* and from ancient times *the things* that are not *yet* done, saying, my council shall stand, and I will do all my *pleasure*."

Now, I submit that if an omnipotent and omniscient God has "declared the end from the beginning," and ordered all "the things that are not yet done" (and you have his word for it here) how is it possible for mortal and finite man to do any thing contrary to the thing ordered, or accomplish any "end" but the one "declared from the beginning?" Here you, who believe in God and the Bible, have his word for it that he has declared all things "from the beginning." Man then *must* do and think as God has declared, and can do nothing else, hence he is *not free*.

The idea that "a man cannot think unless he wills to think" is too preposterous (laying the Bible aside) for any reasonable man to accept who is not a slave to creeds and dogmas. Let "Rationalist," after reading this sentence, stop reading, and assume a quiescent state (for of course *his free will* will enable him to do this)—a state of mental passivity, as it were,—let him *will nothing* for the time being,—and then see if thoughts of some kind do not spontaneously arise in his mind. And then let him *will* to have *no thoughts* for the space of five minutes, and see if the thoughts do not steal into his brain (providing of course he has one) unbidden, and in spite of him—in spite of all his boasted freewill power. Let any reader put this impossible and absurd dictum of "Rationalist" to the test, and he will have a living demonstration in his own brain, which will render any further argument on this point entirely superfluous.

"Rationalist" worries himself into inextricable confusion over causes and effects, first causes, first causes and last effects, etc., etc. Because Ingersoll has said "a first cause is just as impossible as a last effect," Rationalist well nigh swamps himself in a most ludicrous "muss-of-a muddle-of-a-jerry-cum-tumble" of bad diction and worse logic to prove that by such reasoning as Ingersoll's we come to "chaos" and to "nothing," (hasn't the gentleman himself come to chaos if not to nothing?) We reason everything out of existence, he says, and just now we will have left "no nature, no God, no man, no matter" (it would be *no matter* if some *bipids* were gone) "no force," no "nothing"— "literally nothing." Shades of Bacon! let us take breath; for this would certainly be a very bad state of things, from which "good Lord deliver us!" It would be nearly as bad as before the "creation," when nothing existed throughout the infinite realms of space save Jehovah himself.

I will endeavor to make what materialists mean by the impossibility of a first cause or last effect clear to "Rationalist." We believe in one existence, and only one—the universe—which, though never itself having been created or brought into existence (being eternal), is the primal (or "first" if you like) cause of all phenomena Rationalist will thus see that in one sense there is no *first came* as the universe is eternal, yet in another sense there *is* a first cause, viz.: the universe, as it is the primal cause of all phenomena. As to a "last effect," it should be obvious to every *rational* mind that as matter and force are indestructible, and hence eternal in duration, there can be no last effect; for as long as matter and force exist effects must of necessity ensue.

REPLY TO REV. A. J. BRAY

It is a great relief to a Freethinker to find a man among the clergy like Mr. Bray, in point of religious liberality. It is like coming upon an oasis in the waste desert of orthodox bigotry and intolerance.

Mr. Bray is the able editor of the *Canadian Spectator*, of Montreal; and also preaches, I believe, every Sunday in Zion Church in that city. Unlike his clerical brethren generally, when Mr. Ingersoll lectured in Montreal, in April last, Mr. Bray went to hear him, and answered him from his pulpit the two following Sundays. These "Discourses" were published in the succeeding numbers of his paper, the *Spectator*. Hear him on free speech:—

"In a free country all kinds of freedom must be allowed, and Mr. Ingersoll had just as much right to come here and say his say in his own manner, and according to his own discretion, as Mr. Hammond has to come and preach and teach in his way. If men are free to agree with us, they are also free to differ with us; to differ a little, to differ much, to differ altogether. If the Mayor had found a law by which he could prohibit Ingersoll from lecturing against our religious beliefs, I would have started an agitation at once for the repeal of that absurd and antiquated law. If hearing arguments against our faith is likely to unsettle us, then we had better be unsettled. We are badly off with all our religious literature and preaching, if we cannot endure any kind of criticism, and witticism, and argument."

These are brave words, and every fair-minded man in this Dominion will agree with Mr. Bray in his liberal and courageous utterances. They are timely words to go forth in that city where the war of sects has waxed so hot and virulent of late. Montreal needs more men like Bray in her churches, to mollify the bigotry, and stamp out the bitter feuds, and fierce antagonism of Christian against Christian.

As this pamphlet has already reached a much greater length than originally intended, I have but little space to devote to Mr. Bray's Reply to Ingersoll. One or two points, however, must be noticed.

Mr. Bray falls into the same error as "Bystander" in accusing

Ingersoll of attacking a theology which, he tells us, is "opposed to all reason," and now "well nigh obsolete." I would simply say if it is "obsolete," it is the stock in trade of the Christian Church today. Take away from it this obsolete theology (which is "opposed to all reason,") and there is nothing left of Christianity worth speaking of; for the morality Christianity contains does not of right belong to it It is Pagan. It has been *appropriated* by Christianity, and is not original with it. There is not a single moral precept in the Bible, but was taught before that book was written. (For proof of this, see Sir Wm. Jones, Max Muller, Lord Amberly, and "Supernatural Religion.") Therefore, when you take away the dogmas of Christianity—its "obsolete theology"—you take away Christianity itself to all intents and purposes. And hence the utter inconsistency and absurdity of our opponents in taxing us with merely attacking a dead theology, when that dead theology is all there is of a religion which they defend and wish to perpetuate. Seeing, then, that the theology of Christianity is admittedly dead, why not give it up and come over to us? for all you have left—the brotherhood of man—belongs to us: it is our RELIGION OF HUMANITY.

As the only salient point, to my mind, in Mr. Bray's reply to Ingersoll is dealt with in the following letter, which I addressed to the *Spectator*, and which appeared in its columns, I have only space here to reproduce that letter:—

To the Editor of the Canadian Spectator:

Sir,—In your issue of the 10th instant, in a discourse in reply to Col. Ingersoll, I find the following:—

"The lecturer, who seemed to imagine that he understood everything else, was compelled to acknowledge that he did not understand why there should be so much hunger and pain and misery. Why, the world over, life should live upon life. When he has cast Jehovah out of the Universe, he is pained and puzzled to account for the presence of wrong and sorrow. With God he cannot account for it; without God he cannot account for it. If Col. Ingersoll, or any other of that school, can give me an intelligent theory of life, and satisfactory solution of the problem of the presence of evil and pain without God, I am prepared to consider it."

Now, Sir, having the honor (or dishonor, as the case may be,) to belong to that school, I venture to take up the gauntlet thus thrown down. From our stand-point we are able, we think, to give an intelligent theory of these things; and although it may not be wholly devoid of mystery, we claim it is less mysterious than the Christian theory. We claim that the Materialistic explanation of the Universe and its phenomena is more reasonable and less mysterious than the Theistic; and this is why we find ourselves compelled to adopt it and become Atheists. On the Materialistic hypothesis of development and evolution we are certainly *not* "puzzled to account for the presence of wrong and sorrow," however much we may be pained at their fearful prevalence. It is only on the hypothesis of being under the governance of an omnipotent and infinitely *benevolent* Being that we are utterly unable to account for such-a state of things. Although the ultimate tendency of the forces of the-Universe seems to be towards a higher, and higher, and more perfect condition, not only for man, but all animals, and even plants, yet these-forces are, as Science abundantly proves, utterly without mercy—without pity for man or any other animal. Therefore, on the evolution philosophy of things, we can reasonably predicate pain, sorrow, and wrong; and are not puzzled at their existence. It is only on the theory of a *good* God controlling the Universe that we stand dumb with confusion and wonderment in the presence of all this woe, pain, misery, and wrong-with which the world is filled—this terrible "struggle for life," where the-strong prey upon the weak, where animal eats animal, and man eats-man!

The theologians have had upwards of two thousand years to reduce the Materialistic paradoxes of Epicurus on the existence of evil, but have they done so? If there be a God, and He is all-powerful, He *could* remove the *surplus* evil and pain from the world, and if He is all-good He *would* remove it, is an argument which has never yet been answered by a Paley, a Butler, a Dawson, or any other Christian Theist or Bible apologist. I use the phrase "*surplus* evil and pain" for this reason: As a sort of apology for the rank malevolence abroad in the world, and as an argument for the existence of a beneficent God, Christian Theists tell us that pain is necessary as an antecedent to the proper enjoyment of pleasure; that it is necessary to the growth and development of character; that the storm of the ocean is an essential pre-requisite to the adequate enjoyment of the subsequent calm; that all smooth sailing would be monotonous and insipid. Now, we will admit this for the sake of the argument; but there yet remains the mass of *surplus* evil to be accounted for, which is wholly unnecessary for such corrective and distributive purposes. It may, perhaps, be necessary that the tempest toss the ship about on the bosom of the ocean in order that the living freight may have a keener appreciation of the succeeding calm, and also to develop awe and sublimity in their breasts; but to accomplish this it is scarcely to the purpose to send all to the bottom of the ocean! That we may have a proper relish for our food and a due appreciation of the blessings of a good appetite, it may be necessary that we feel the pangs of hunger and starvation occasionally; but to give us this wholesome discipline it would seem hardly necessary that millions of human beings should actually be starved to death!

Now, on the theory of *inexorable law** instead of a *beneficent Providence*, we are not surprised that a ship which is not strong enough to ride the storm should go to the bottom, even though five hundred bishops and clergymen be aboard supplicating an unknown God for succor. On the theory of inexorable and merciless law in which we are fast bound, we are not "puzzled" that millions of human beings should starve to death when these laws or conditions of Nature are violated in over-population and a false political and social economy. Or when a Tay bridge goes down with its living freight under the pressure of train and tempest, the Atheist is neither surprised nor puzzled: but the Christian, who worships a benevolent (?) God and believes that not a hair falls from his head without His notice, can only look at such a malevolent horror in dumb silence and amazement—he has no explanation. Our theory of the presence of evil in the world is, therefore, at least rational; but, is the Christian theory rational? Is it rational to-suppose that all the pain, sorrow, and evil in the world have been caused by the puerile circumstance of a woman eating an apple? This would be as monstrously unjust as it is irrational and absurd.

As to the origin and maintenance of life "without God," it is quite as comprehensible and rational without God as with one with the Christian conditions and qualifications. An universe of matter containing the "promise and potency of all forms and qualities of life" is as intelligible and comprehensible as a God *outside* the Universe embodying the potency of all life. From the time that Lucretius declared that "Nature is seen to do all things spontaneously of herself without the meddling of the Gods," and Bruno that matter is the "universal mother who brings forth all things as the fruit of her own womb," down to Prof. Tyndall, who discerns in matter "the promise and potency of every form and quality of life," scientists have never been able to discover the least intrusion of any creative power into the operations of

** Materialists, in using the phrase "law of Nature," use a popular expression, but not in the popular sense as presupposing a law-giver. By "law of Nature" we simply mean natural sequence—the uniformity of Nature's operations.*

Nature and the affairs of this world, or the least trace of interference by any God or gods. In the primeval ages of ignorance and barbarism the gods were supposed to do everything, from the production of wind, rain, tempest, thunder and lightning, earthquakes, &c, down to dyspepsia and potato-bugs. Science now explains all these things and a thousand others. Indeed, in modern philosophy there is no room for the gods in the Universe, and nothing left for them to do. And there cannot be any room *beyond* it for them, for "above Nature we cannot rise."

The Materialistic theory (and to it we subscribe) is that there is but *one existence,* the *Universe,* and that it is eternal—without beginning or end—that the matter of the Universe never could have been created, for *ex nihilo nihil fit,* (from nothing nothing can come,) and that it contains within itself the potency adequate to the production of all phenomena. This we think to be more conceivable and intelligent than the Christian theory that there are two existences—God and the Universe—and that there was a time when there was but one existence, God, and that after an indefinite period of quiescence and "masterly inactivity" He finally created a Universe either out of Himself or out of nothing—either one of which propositions is philosophically absurd. And in either case, to say that God would be infinite would be equally absurd.

Respectfully,

ALLEN PRINGLE.

Napanee, Ont., April 23, 1880.

THE OATH QUESTION

(TO CANADIAN FREETHINKERS.)

As this Pamphlet will be widely circulated throughout Canada (especially Ontario), it will come into the hands of most Canadian Freethinkers, and I have therefore thought this an opportune time to bring this question, in which we are all so deeply interested, before the Freethinkers of Canada, and urge upon them the necessity of agitation for reform. The time has come, I think, for action in petitioning Parliament to remove the serious and most unjust disabilities under which we, as a class, are now placed, and thus have equal rights extended to all citizens. As the law now stands we are deprived of our rights in the courts, and the ends of justice are often defeated, not only to our detriment but that of Christians themselves. If the presiding judge choose to adhere to the strict letter of the law the testimony of Atheists is refused. It is very easy to see how the gravest injustice could be inflicted upon Freethinkers and Christians alike under this unjust law. A Freethinker may be the only witness to a case involving the interests of a Christian, or he may be the only witness for himself as against a Christian; and by his not being eligible as a witness the ends of justice are defeated. Or an unscrupulous believer may claim that he is a Freethinker to get rid of giving evidence altogether. It is true there seems to rest with the Judges a large amount of discretionary power as to whom they will or will not accept to give evidence; and the majority, perhaps, of our Canadian Judges exhibit a commendable spirit of liberality in the matter of accepting the testimony of Freethinkers. But occasionally one is to be met with, too full of religion and bigotry to recognize our rights or extend any discretion in our favor. In the city of Toronto, a few months ago, the testimony of two respectable and intelligent witnesses was refused because they did not believe the dogmas of the popular religion.* As an offset to this, however, an Ottawa-Judge recently showed his fairness and liberality by allowing a Juryman Freethinker, who declined to take the oath, to make an affirmation. The Grand Juror referred to, Mr. John Law, of Ottawa, is described as-a gentleman of "unimpeachable honor and probity," and hence his simple affirmation being, as he stated, fully binding on his conscience, would, or certainly ought to, have more weight than the oaths of many witnesses (believers) who are taken into the witness box. The presiding Judge, doubtless, so regarded the matter, and therefore, in his discretion, magnanimously allowed Mr. Law to affirm.

In England, under "The Evidence Amendment Act" of 1869,32* and 33 Vic, c. 68, s. 4, Atheists can make the following affirmation instead of taking the Christian oath, and the Court must allow all Freethinkers to do so who demand it:

"I solemnly promise and declare that the evidence given by me to the Court, shall be the truth, the whole truth, and nothing but the truth."

We want a similar Act in Canada, and then Counsel will not be able as now to badger witnesses about "infidel belief," and turn the court into an inquisition; nor will a bigoted judge have it in his discretion to order Atheists down from the witness-box as not fit to give evidence. At almost every sitting of our courts it is demonstrated beyond a doubt. that believers in the Bible, who take the oath on that Book, do not all tell the truth under oath. Every judge and lawyer in the land knows this, and all know it who have much to do in courts of law. The simple word or affirmation of an honest man, whether Christian or Infidel, is better than a thousand oaths of many believers in the Bible, who are without hesitation taken into the witness-box. Moreover, the Atheist in making the above affirmation under the Act referred to, is subject to the same penalties for perjury as the Christian is in taking, the usual oath. There is, therefore, no good reason why we should! not have a similar Act here, and it behooves us to begin to move towards its consummation. Freethinkers are getting numerous in Canada, and they are, to say the least, as exemplary citizens, socially and morally, as their Christian neighbors? Why then should they be longer denied equal rights with their Christian neighbors?

** Since writing this I have been informed by one of the witnesses alluded to, that no blame can be fairly imputed to the presiding Judge in this case, as he felt compelled, against his sympathies, to carry out the unjust law.*

In England they still have a State Religion, yet the rights of Rationalists in this respect are conceded to them. Here we have no state religion, and yet we suffer under religious disabilities which are utterly out of keeping with the spirit of the age, and which are fast being swept away in every civilized country. The Bradlaugh imbroglio recently in the English House of Commons has had the effect of opening some people's eyes, especially those conservative Christians who are still afflicted with lingerings of that bigoted, intolerant, and persecuting spirit which formerly lighted the fires of Smithfleld, hung quakers, imprisoned so-called "blasphemers," and violated civil contracts in the name of God. In the last election in England, a few months ago, Charles Bradlaugh, the eminent Atheist and Republican, was elected to the English House of Commons for the borough of Northampton, and in entering the House he claimed his right, instead of taking the Parliamentary oath, to affirm under the Act referred to above. The House at first refused, vacillated, appointed Committees, and vigorously debated the matter; while the bigoted members at once proceeded to unbudget themselves in true Christian style against the "vermin" Atheist. Meanwhile the levelheaded Atheist knew what he was about, and, as the sequel showed, proved himself more than a match for the English House of Commons. Meanwhile also, the people of England—the working classes—were-watching the whole business, and finally when Bradlaugh was refused both oath and affirmation, and the intention to keep the Atheist out of Parliament became manifest, they (the people) promptly came to the front. Just then it began to dawn on "the powers that be" that *vox populi, vox Dei* had more truth than poetry in it. The people of England—the producers—(called "lower classes" by the "upper" *non*-producers) assembled in scores of thousands in indignation mass-meetings all over England, demanding the admission of Charles Bradlaugh (their best friend) to his rightful seat in the English House of Commons. The aforesaid "powers that be" took the alarm. Seeing that the "voice of the people" was even more potent than the "voice of God," they prudently bowed to its mandate. They perceived that no Clock Tower, or other tower in England would hold the workingman's friend even for the space of seven days. Bradlaugh must be released or the House of Brunswick might peradventure soon be in mourning—not, probably, for spilled blood, but for a crown, aye, a crown! No wonder the English Government feared to see Charles Bradlaugh enter the House of Commons. He had impeached the House of Brunswick. And it was no "soft impeachment." No, but a terribly hard indictment! Was it ever answered? No, it was too true to answer. The only answer was from Lord Randolph Churchill in the House of Commons, and it was characteristic. This rabid monarchist, with much more Christian zeal than knowledge or discretion, took Bradlaugh's "Impeachment of the House of Brunswick" and cast it viciously under his feet on the floor of the House of Commons. That was the way the "Impeachment" was answered! Well, as Shakspeare says, "let the galled jades wince!" But the Atheist had his revenge! They had put him in the Tower, but they very soon let him out. He had been somewhat accustomed to fighting the English Government, having beaten them twice, and he feared not. He was imprisoned one day, but released the next. An Act was speedily passed giving more even than Bradlaugh at first demanded—giving every member who wishes in future, the right to affirm instead of taking the Christian Oath. Bradlaugh has accordingly made his affirmation as he at first demanded, and has taken his seat in the English House of Commons as M. P. for Northampton,* And now let every Freethinker throughout the civilized world rejoice, for this is a great victory for our cause! The eloquent champion of our dearest rights has achieved a glorious victory on the very threshold of the English Parliament before he enters it! Let us take courage! The indomitable and invincible Iconoclast has now attained a position where his voice will be heard in behalf of liberty and the rights of man the world over! He is called "coarse" by some over-cultured people, but his coarseness is of the kind the world needs, and therefore *we* do not object to it. The superstitions, and errors, and wrongs, and oppressions still weighing down our fellow-men need bare-handed ("coarse") handling, without gloves, and Bradlaugh wears none of these, but fearlessly throws down the gauntlet to falsehood and oppression whenever and wherever found. But I fear I am getting a little off the Oath Question here in my enthusiasm for Charles Bradlaugh, Member of Parliament for Northampton.

* *The press of Canada, with very few exceptions, have done Mr. Bradlaugh a great injustice in connection with the oath question, as they have (perhaps unintentionally) utterly misrepresented him. They have charged that he "flaunted his Atheism before the House of Commons," that he at first refused to take the oath on conscientious grounds and subsequently "swallowed his scruples" and offered to take*

the oath; and that, therefore, the Atheist is without conscience and without principle, sacrificing all for place. Now, this is all utterly untrue. He did not flaunt his Atheism before the House. He did not refuse to take the oath, but simply claimed to be allowed to affirm. The Speaker having intimated to Mr. Bradlaugh that if he desired to address the House in explanation of his claim he would be permitted to do so, Mr. Bradlaugh said, "I have repeatedly, for nine years past, made an affirmation in the highest courts of jurisdiction in this realm: I am ready to make such a declaration or affirmation." And subsequently when Mr. Bradlaugh offered to take the oath, it was after he had made an explanation that although a portion of it to him was a meaningless form, yet that the oath as a whole, if he took it would be binding on his conscience substantially the same as an affirmation. These are the facts, all taken from authentic official sources, and not from what bigoted and prejudiced correspondents have sent us across the ocean. My authority is the record of the proceedings of the Parliamentary Committees on the Bradlaugh case, where the facts I have stated were distinctly brought out in evidence, to which source I beg to refer the newspapers of this country and call upon them to make the amende honorable by setting this matter right before their readers.

In conclusion, I beg to again urge upon my fellow Freethinkers throughout Canada the necessity of taking such action as will secure for us our legal rights in the Courts of this country. I trust that the petitions to Parliament for an Evidence Amendment Act, which we design ere long to put in circulation, may be numerously signed and diligently circulated by the liberal friends in the various places to which they will be sent.

Selby, Lennox Co., Ont., July, 1880

"It can do truth no service to blink the fact, known to all who have the most ordinary Acquaintance with literary history, that a large portion, of the noblest and most valuable moral teaching has been the work, not only of men who did not know, but of men who knew and rejected, the Christian faith."—J. S. Mill.

"The history of Christ is contained in records which exhibit contradictions that cannot be reconciled, imperfections that would greatly detract from even admitted human compositions, and erroneous principles of morality that would hardly have found a place in the most incomplete system of the philosophers of Greece and Rome."—Rev. Dr. Giles.

"That any human creature, be he peer or peasant, man or woman, pauper or millionaire, should be visited with pains and penalties because of his or her speculative opinion on a subject whereon but few even of professing Christians are agreed, is a bitter satire on our vaunted liberty. My Lords, it is the spirit which lighted the martyr-fires of Smithfield, and led to the stake gallant and noble souls such as Bruno. It is a noble; company you are placing me in, my Lords, and I shall thank you for it."—*Ibid.*

"Who shall number the patient and earnest seekers after truth, from the days of Galileo until now, whose lives have been embittered, and their good name blasted, by the mistaken zeal of Bibliolators? Who shall count the host of weaker men whose sense of truth has been destroyed in the effort to harmonize impossibilities—whose life has been wasted in the attempt to force the generous new wine of Science into the old bottles of Judaism, compelled by the outcry of the same strong party." *Prof. Huxley.*

"Thou shalt not kill, even the smallest creature.

"Thou shalt not appropriate to thyself what belongs to another.

"Thou shalt not infringe the laws of chastity.

"Thou shalt not lie.

"Thou shalt not calumniate.

"Thou shalt not speak of injuries.

"Thou shalt not excite quarrels, by repeating the words of others.

"Thou shalt not hate."

—*Moral Precepts from Buddhistic Sacred Books.*

"I discern in matter * * the promise and potency of all forms and qualities of life."—*Tyndall*

"A poor man, in our day, has many gods foisted on him; and big voices bid him 'Worship or be ————' in a menacing and confusing manner. What shall he do? By far the greater part of said gods, current in the public, whether canonized by Pope or Populas, are mere dumb asses and beautiful prize-oxen—nay, some of them, who have articulate faculty, are devils instead of Gods. A poor man that would save his soul alive is reduced to the sad necessity of *sharply trying his gods* whether they are divine or not, which is a terrible pass for mankind, and lays an awful problem upon each man."—*Tomas Carlyle*

"These Gospels, so important to the Church, have not come to us in one undisputed form. We have no authorised copy of them in their original language, so that we may know in what precise words they were originally written. The authorities from which we derive their sacred text are various ancient copies, written by hand on parchment. Of the Gospels there are more than five hundred of these manuscripts of various ages, from the fourth century after Christ to the fifteenth, when printing superseded manual writing for publication of books. Of these five hundred and more, *no two* are in all points alike: probably in no two of the more ancient can *even a few consecutive verses* be found in which all the words agree."—*Dean Alford. "How to Study the New Testament."*

"I find Armenian Christians who say that it is a sin to eat a hare; Greeks who affirm that the Holy Ghost does not proceed from the Son; Nestorians who deny that Mary is the mother of God: Latins who boast that in the extreme West the Christians of Europe think quite contrary to those of Asia and Africa. I know that ten or twelve sects in Europe anathematise each other; the Musselmen disdain the Christians, whom they nevertheless tolerate; the Jews hold in equal execration the Christians and Muselmen; the Fire-worshippers despise them all; the remnant of the Sabeans will not eat with either of the Other sects; and the Brahmin cannot suffer either Salbeans, or Fire-Worshippers, or Christians, or Musselmen, or Jews. I have a hundred times wished that Jesus Christ, in coming to be incarnated in Judea, had united all the sects under his laws. I have asked myself why, being God, he did not use the rights of his divinity; why, in coming to deliver us from sin, he has left us in sin; why, in coming to enlighten all men, he has left almost all men in darkness. I know I am nothing; I know that from the depth of my nothingness I have no right to interrogate the Being of Beings; but I may, like Job, raise a voice of respectful sorrow from the bosom of my misery."—*Voltaire.*